Aspects of modern sociology

Social research

GENERAL EDITORS

John Barron Mays
Eleanor Rathbone Professor of Sociology, University of Liverpool

Maurice Craft
Senior Lecturer in Education, University of Exeter

A History of
Social Research Methods

Gary Easthope, M.A. (Soc.), Ph. D.

Lecturer in Sociology
The University of East Arglia

Longman

Longman
1724-1974

LONGMAN GROUP LIMITED
London

Associated companies, branches and representatives throughout the world

© Longman Group Limited 1974

First published 1974

ISBN 0 582 48480·4 cased
         48481·2 paper

*Printed in Hong Kong
by Dai Nippon Printing Co., (H.K.) Ltd.*

Contents

Editors' Preface

The first series in Longman's *Aspects of Modern Sociology* library was concerned with the social structure of modern Britain, and was intended for students following professional and other courses in universities, polytechnics, colleges of education, and elsewhere in further and higher education, and well as for those members of a wider public wishing to pursue an interest in the nature and structure of British society.

This second series sets out to examine the history, aims, techniques and limitations of social research, and it is hoped that it will be of interest to the same readership. It will seek to offer an informative but not uncritical introduction to some of the methodologies of social science.

JOHN BARRON MAYS
MAURICE CRAFT

Acknowledgements

We are grateful to the following for permission to reproduce copyright material:
The Author and the American Sociological Association for an extract from 'Sociology of Empirical Social Research' by P.F. Lazarsfeld, as appeared in *ASR*, Vol 27, pp. 757-767; Tavistock Publications Ltd for a diagram from *American Sociological Review* Vol 15, 1950 by R.F. Bales and two diagrams from *The Origins of Scientific Sociology*, 1963 by J. Madge on pages 258 & 452; Columbia University Press for a diagram and extracts from *The People's Choice* by P.F. Lazarsfeld; Commonwealth Fund for a table from *Unraveling Juvenile Delinquency*, 1950 by S. & E. Glueck; Holt, Rinehart and Winston, Inc., New York for fig. 4 Horseplay, in 'An Experimental Study of Leadership and Group Life' by Ronald Lippitt and Ralph K. White from *Readings in Social Psychology* ed. by Eleanor E. Maccoby, Theodore M. Newcomb and Eugene L. Hartley. (c) 1947, 1952, 1958; Macmillan, London and Basingstoke for extracts and tables from *Life and Labour of the People of London* by C. Booth; Routledge & Kegan Paul Ltd and Macmillan Publishing Co., Inc for a table and extract from *Suicide* by Emile Durkheim. Copyright 1952 by The Free Press, a Corporation; The Journal Press and Dr. Lippitt for fig 5, p. 285 from "Patterns of aggressive behaviour in experimentally created 'Social climate'", by Kurt Lewin, Ronald Lippitt and Ralph K. White which appeared in *The Journal of Social Psychology*, 1939, 10, 271-299; The University of Chicago Press for a diagram from *Juvenile Delinquency and Urban Areas* by C.R. Shaw & H.D. McKay. (c) 1942, 1969, 1972

Introduction

> Most authors write as if they are the first to explore their subjects. They fail to take advantage of the insights of previous investigators. They don't even know of their existence. . . . There are many rewards to be derived from consulting the maps of previous explorers, even though these charts require correction and redrawing. In short, we need, in sociology, a better regard for our own past accomplishments.
>
> H. Alpert (1963) discussing manuscripts submitted to him as editor of the *American Sociological Review*.

This book is not primarily a history of social research. It is not a history because my concern is not with a sequence of research projects and their chronological ordering, although this is dealt with, but with the basic orientations of the sociologists who carried out these research projects. It does not deal with social research in its entirety because to do so would be to write a history of sociology. Duncan Mitchell's *A Hundred Years of Sociology* (1968) already fulfils this function. Nor does it deal with the links between theory and methods for this also has been admirably covered in John Madge's book *The Origins of Scientific Sociology* (1963). The book focuses instead on the narrow field of research methods: the experiment, the survey, participant observation, life histories, the comparative method and the problems of measurement and analysis associated with each of these methods of collecting information about the social world. It focuses also on social research in the United States of America, because although the methods of social research were invented in Europe their development was almost entirely accomplished in America.

To point out its limited focus on research methods is not the same as saying that the book is limited. A narrow beam has the advantage of making us look more closely at what we can see. What we do see is that the social research methods we use today were not an arbitrary growth. They had their origins in the revolutionary changes in society that were associated also with the growth of sociology. Chapter 1 deals with these origins and demonstrates that sociology and social research methods were both products of the attempt to understand and control the social world by the use of science. Understanding was sought through participant observation and understanding and control were sought in the use of the survey, the experiment and the comparative method. Chapters 2 to 5 deal with the development of each of these methods in turn and that development is traced in each chapter by looking in detail at specific pieces of research which were important in the development of a method. Chapter 6 uses the same technique to look at measurement and analysis. In the final chapter, Chapter 7, it is argued that the development of sociology led to a break with its origins; that the conception of sociology as a means to control the world was abandoned and sociologists concentrated instead on understanding the world by the use of science. Some possible reasons for the abandonment of the notion of control are given and it is argued that such a stance is not possible in sociology: men, unlike physical objects, are self-aware. This self-awareness means that the predictions and descriptions of sociologists of the social world are not separate from that social world but form part of it. This implies that there can never be any recurrent situations to study in sociology because study of a situation changes that situation. Thus sociology can never be a science and must always cause change. This lays a duty on the sociologist to make ethical decisions about the direction he wishes such change to go rather than leave such decisions to others.

This history of social research calls then for a reappraisal of the criteria by which we choose our research methods. We need, as sociologists, to look at our research methods not only in terms of how scientific they are but also in terms of the ethical assumptions implicit in them. When we look at our research methods in this light we may well decide that the comparative method and participant observation, often criticised for their non-scientific nature, need to be reconsidered as sociological methods of equal importance, if not more importance, than the survey or the experiment. Sociology and its methods was in its origins concerned not only with understanding the social world but with controlling or changing it. Sociology today has the same two goals. A conservative sociology would be concerned with controlling the changes in social life, a radical sociology with changing the social world. It is inherent in the nature of sociology that both must intervene in the processes of the social world. That intervention, whether for control or change, can itself be seen as a commitment to freedom. To make men aware of the constraints upon their actions, to point out the consequences of their decisions, is to give them a greater freedom of choice in the way they live their lives.

The origins of sociology 1

It being impossible not to observe a growing distrust of mere
hypothetical theory and *a priori* assumption, and the appearance of
a general conviction that, in the business of social science, principles
are valid for application only inasmuch as they are legitimate
induction from facts, accurately observed and methodically classified.

Journal of the Statistical Society of London (1838)

Change can do little for us, except make us victims, until we are able
to observe it. But observing it we can do little to control it, until we
can measure it.

Smith and White (1929, p. 236.)

The concept of sociology as a social science arose at the beginning
of the nineteenth century. The concept of such a science of society
arose firstly because a new philosophical idea emerged and
dominated philosophical thought, and secondly because society
changed rapidly and drastically. The idea that emerged was that
of rationality. Sociology arose from the idea of rationality and
the changes in society. If rationality was to be the keynote of
philosophical thought what more natural than to apply that
rationality to the chaotic changing world around the philosopher?
Out of this coincidence emerged the idea of a science of society:
the application of rationality to the study of society. From this
coincidence of the idea of rationality and the changes in society
arose also the methods of sociology. These methods may be listed
as the experiment, the survey, observation and life histories, the
comparative method of looking at history and the various means
of measurement and analysis of the collected facts about society.
Their origins in the nineteenth century are discussed in this

chapter. Before discussing origins, however, it is necessary to look at the emergence of the idea of sociology as a science of society. This brief examination of the emergence of sociology as a discipline is necessary because the methods of sociology as well as being the products of the ideas of the nineteenth century, and the interaction of the ideas and the society, are also a product of the concept of sociology that emerged from that process.

THE IDEA OF A SCIENCE OF SOCIETY

The idea of a science of society implies three things: first that there is an entity called society which is not the same as the sum of the individuals in it (this point was not fully met until Durkheim wrote his *Rules of Sociological Method* in 1895 but it is implied in the concept of a science of society); secondly that the processes occurring in society are not known; and thirdly that society can be understood by the methods of science.

Why did men believe in an entity that was more than the sum of the individuals in it? The industrial and political revolutions of that time both celebrated the freedom of the individual from traditional ties and bonds. One might expect therefore a science of individuals, psychology, rather than a science of society. However, although both revolutions celebrated the individual their effect was to produce what has been called mass society. The industrial revolution massed men in factories and into terraced housing, and separated workers from other classes in a way which differed radically from the previous separation of classes in the countryside. The French Revolution treated all men as citizens of the nation, equal before the law, rather than distinguishing between individuals in terms of their religion and background. (The revolution did of course distinguish violently between the aristocrats and others initially but eventually all became nominally equal.)

Why did intellectuals believe they did not understand the processes of this society? The brief answer is that the social world changed dramatically at this time so that old understandings were no longer useful. The political world also changed dramatically in the French Revolution. The importance for a science of society of the Revolution was that it made men believe they could control their world and that this world was not immutably fixed by tradition. To control that world they had to first understand it. For that understanding they turned to science.

Why did the intellectuals of the day turn to science for explanation and prediction of the new social world? Again a brief answer would be that the industrial and political revolutions had removed traditional authority, so men sought a new authority. They found that authority in the rationalism of science which had been so successful in predicting events in the physical world.

These brief answers to difficult questions sketch the outline of the argument that sociology emerged as a coincidence between changes in society and the idea of rationality. It is necessary to go more deeply into the argument and answer the questions in greater detail. The idea that there existed an entity called society may be traced to the distinction between the state and society that had arisen in German philosophical thought. The state in German medieval philosophy was seen as the source of authority and was vested in the person of the king. The concept of society was originally introduced as a technical term to explain and justify the middle-class burghers' attempts to assert their rights against the king. It was however through the social contract philosophers, Hobbes and Locke, that the conception of the separation of the political from the social came into the mainstream of European thought. These men, who were involved in a polemical debate about men's rights to obey or revolt against governments, in the course of their arguments distinguished between the political and the social worlds: Hobbes saw political society as a union of men, not as any particular type of government, and Locke suggested that men may revolt against government to preserve society. This separation of the political from the social was reinforced by the men Manuel (1965) calls the Prophets of Paris. These philosophers, of whom Comte is the most famous, concerned themselves with the social world but not the political world. Their reasons for this may have been the rapid changes that occurred in politics which seemed to lack relation to the slower changes in society—*plus ca change, plus c'est la meme chose* referred to the revolutions of 1848 but it is applicable to 1800 also.

Distinction between political and social factors may explain the emphasis on society rather than politics in the thought of the day but it still does not explain why society was explained in terms of groups rather than individuals. We need to look at the consequences of the industrialisation of Europe and of the French Revolution. Industrialisation had produced cities as unlike previous cities as those had been unlike the villages which had preceded them. These cities had massed together large numbers of people. Unlike the situation in the countryside where people were known as individuals who belonged to a class, in the city they were known only in terms of class. They were perceived as a group rather than as individuals who belonged to a group: 'a factory worker' rather than 'Woolacott the farm labourer'. Perceptions of groups, acting as groups, stressed the collective nature of society rather than the nature of the individuals in that society. This does not imply that there were no psychological theories of society that talked of man's innate aggression or his innate rationality. These still existed but the tendency to see society as composed of groups rather than individuals was there and was to receive intellectual backing from Marx's analysis of history. Changes in politics, like changes in society, had also taken away the individuality of men. The liberating effects of the new equality were greatly applauded but a few thinkers; de Tocqueville in particular, saw the levelling effect of democracy and its possible tendency to mediocrity and the tyranny of the mass:

> Whenever social conditions are equal, public opinion presses with enormous weight upon the mind of each individual; it surrounds, directs and oppresses him. ... As men grow more alike, each man feels himself weaker in regard to all the rest; as he discerns nothing by which he is considerably raised above them or distinguished from them, he mistrusts himself as soon as they assail him ... he is instantly overwhelmed by the sense of his own insignificance and weakness. (1945 edn, ii 261)

The result of these social and political changes was a conception of society as a collection of groups rather than as a collection of individuals.

These same social and political changes led men to realise that they did not understand the social world around them. Change was rapid and revolutionary. The guidelines for social behaviour which had been sufficient for centuries, and the institutions regulating behaviour which had been effective for centuries, were no longer capable of dealing with the new society which emerged from the chaos of the industrial and political revolutions. The social world became an unknown area where old ideas failed to make sense. The magnitude of this change can be appreciated when it is realised that there have only been two major economic revolutions in the history of man. The first was the agrarian revolution when men changed from a predominantly nomadic hunting way of life to one of agricultural settlement; the second was the industrial revolution when men changed from a rural to an urban existence. Urban centres had formed before the industrial revolution but they were small and few. The new industrial cities were large and there were many more of them. New modes of social life developed new patterns of behaviour which were not understandable in terms of old categories. The working classes in particular presented a great unknown. To the middle classes of the day they were. as remote from normal understanding as primitive tribesmen, as this quotation from Mayhew (1851) shows:

> Almost every tribe of people who have submitted themselves to social laws, recognising the rights of property and reciprocal social duties, and thus acquiring wealth and forming themselves into a respectable caste, are surrounded by hordes of vagabonds and outcasts from their own community . . .
>
> It is curious that no one has as yet applied the above facts (concerning the relations between settled peoples and those who surround them) to the explanation of certain anomalies in the present state of society among ourselves. That we, like the Kaffirs, Fellahs, and Finns, are surrounded by wandering hordes . . . paupers, beggars,

and outcasts, possessing nothing but what they acquire by depreda-
tion from the industrious, provident, and civilised portion of the
community—that the heads of these nomads are remarkable for the
greater development of the jaws and cheekbones rather than those
of the head—and that they have a secret language of their own ...
for the concealment of their designs: these are points of coincidence
so striking that, when placed before the mind, make us marvel
that the analogy should have remained thus long unnoticed. (i,
1–2).

To understand the unknown, to order the chaos of change,
thinkers developed a series of concepts that remain to this day
the key concepts of sociology: community, authority, class, the
sacred, rationality, alienation, anomie. These concepts were
philosophically conservative because they sought to find order in
change, and order is conservative in its implications.

This search for order was related to the idea of sociology as a
science. A science seeks recurrent patterns, regularities and order
so that predictions can be made. Science proceeds on the assumption of repetitive patterns in nature—if A caused B yesterday
it will cause B tomorrow. However although the concepts were
concepts of order they were artistic rather than scientific in conception. The early sociologists 'were not working with finite and
ordered problems in front of them. They were not problem-
solving at all. Each was, with deep intuition, with profound
imaginative grasp, reacting to the world around him, even as does
the artist, and, also like the artist, objectifying internal and only
partly conscious, states of mind' (Nisbet, 1957 p. 19).

The idea of sociology as a science of society was not therefore
implicit in its concepts. This did not, nor does it, preclude sociology
from a claim to be scientific; the concepts of natural science are
equally artistic in their grasp of the world. Science is a method
of validating those concepts, it is not the concepts themselves.
.Where then did the idea of sociology as a science derive? It
derived from the social contract ideas of rational man, taking
decisions rationally arrived at; rationality has always been the
brother of science. It came also from the success of the natural

sciences. They stood as a model of precise thinking and successful prediction to be imitated.

Another element in the adoption of science came from the decline of the old values and interpretations. Theology after the Reformation no longer gave men their rules for living. Humanism, the method of deriving rules for society from the writings of the ancients, no longer seemed applicable in a society that had changed so drastically, politically and socially. The only alternative left was that of the scientific mode of thought. But the use of science implies treating men as 'things', as 'objects', as 'variables' in the experiment. How was it possible to take this view? The answer lies once again in the growth of the industrial city. The industrial city already treated men as objects, men were called factory hands as though all that was important about them was their hands. The working classes were seen as inferior and so could be treated like objects. In our own day the consequences of treating men as not fully human is only too apparent—Hitler's Germany, like nineteenth-century Europe, was able to treat people as objects. The cities also meant a new relationship between people. In a city people met hundreds of others daily. It was not, and is not, possible to treat all of them as individuals. This was as true for the middle classes amongst themselves as it was for the working classes. The industrial city brought together large numbers of middle-class people who did not enter into personal relationships with all the others as they would have done in a small town. This led to a detachment from others, a minimal involvement that also encourages the treatment of others as objects. All these elements coalesced into the positivist philosophy of Comte: 'The method which has triumphed in mathematics, astronomy, physics, chemistry and biology must eventually prevail in politics and culminate in the founding of a positive science of society, which is called sociology.' (cited in Aron 1968).

The idea of a science of society emerged as men began to conceive of an entity separate from the state which they called 'society'. As they realised that because of the rapid political and social changes that were occurring they did not understand the workings of that society, they sought understanding through the use of the scientific method. These same changes can be related not only to the rise of a science of society but to the rise of the methods used by that science.

THE METHODS OF SOCIOLOGY

The origins of a science of society are also the origins of the methods used by that science. It would be surprising if this was not the case. Following from the insight given by that statement it is possible to disentangle the apparent chaotic jumble of research methods that are at present being used in sociology. It allows an order to be imposed on chaos. It gives a distinction between the experiment, the survey, observation, comparative method and analysis that relies not only on their present differences but on their origins. Having created an order, a pattern, from which distinctions between research methods can be made, it becomes possible to look at the development of each method in turn. However it must be realised that this order, this outline, is only a guide. Both in the origins of each method and their use there are a complex of variables: surveys and observations share a common origin as ways to study the urban poor and a survey is, after all, only an observation of many pieces of behaviour which are often verbal. Having made that caveat, let us proceed to look at the origins of each method in turn, remembering that the origins of one method may be equally valid for the next.

The experiment

Of all the methods of sociology perhaps the experiment is the most 'scientific'. The experimental method is often taken to mean the same as the scientific method. It is from the desire to be like the natural sciences that experiments in sociology arise. And yet there have been few experiments in sociology. The reasons for this are theoretical, practical and ethical. The experimental method demands that all variables be controlled except the experimental variable. To achieve this requires an agreement on what are the significant variables in the experiment. This in turn requires what Kuhn (1962) calls a paradigm: an overarching approach to the world that blinkers and limits the scientists' viewpoint, that reduces a problem to a puzzle. Like a puzzle a scientific problem operates within a set of rules, an agreement to pretend. A good analogy might be that of a chess problem: within the rules of chess there is opportunity to be creative, to tax the mind, but the rules remain. One can win at chess by reaching over and lifting the opponent's pieces at any time, or more drastically one can disable or kill an opponent (Garfinkel, 1967, gives an interesting account of such challenges to the rules), but to do this is to break the rules and make the game meaningless. The rules of the scientific game are the paradigm ruling at any particular historical time. This may be Newtonian physics or Einstein's relativity. Whatever paradigm is accepted forms the rules within which the game is played. Sociology has no such agreed paradigm. Kuhn's (1962) comment on early physical optics is applicable to sociology today:

> Being able to take no common body of belief for granted, each writer on physical optics felt forced to build his field anew from its foundations. In doing so, his choice of supporting observation and experiment was relatively free, for there was no standard set of methods or of phenomena that every optical writer felt forced to employ and explain. Under these circumstances, the dialogue of the resulting books was often directed as much to the members of other schools as it was to nature. That pattern is not unfamiliar in a number of creative fields today, nor is it incompatible with significant discovery and invention. (p. 13).

Lacking a paradigm it is impossible to decide which variables are important, or even to decide which are the variables. It is therefore extremely difficult to conduct experiments. The practical and ethical problems are easier to explain. In practical terms it would be very difficult to conduct, let us say, a revolution controlling all the variables except the experimental one. The ethical problems involved in such a procedure are also apparent.

These difficulties, theoretic, practical and ethical, have not meant that there have been no experiments in sociology. Experiments have taken place of two types. The first type of experiment has taken place largely in the subfield known as social psychology. Small groups present no insurmountable practical problems for study and although ethical problems remain it is easier to justify changing groups by external interference than it is to justify changing complete societies. The second type of experiment has only recently become possible with the advent of the computer. This is the whole field of study known under the title of simulation. Societies can be studied in this way by abstracting variables and seeing how they interact within the paradigm of the idea of system. The idea of abstracting variables from individual and unique situations and manipulating them independently of context was first put forward by Simmel (1902) in the early years of this century, but the full impact of the idea had to await the advent of the computer.

The survey

The experiment may be said to be derived from the idea of sociology as a science. In contrast the method that for many people characterises sociology was not developed for scientific purposes at all, but for administrative and compassionate reasons. The administrative origins of the survey overlap with the origins of statistics and are therefore discussed in the section on measurement and analysis (p. 120).

What then were the compassionate reasons for the origins of the survey? The compassion was for the urban poor of the industrial cities. The survey developed as an attempt to illustrate the misery and degradation of these people. This method of detailed compilation of facts was an attempt to convince others, particularly administrators, of the need for action. Go to the public, or the government, and show them the misery of the poor and they would deny it. They preferred to believe that what was reported was exaggerated or untypical and even if convinced it was typical they still blamed those concerned for not helping themselves. Engels (1845) spent boundless energy trying to show people that

13

what he had found was typical. Booth (1892) went further than Engels. Engels, having proved the extent of poverty, accepted Marx's philosophical analysis of its causes. Booth was not willing to accept philosophical analysis of causes and looked for the causes of poverty, as well as its extent, in the data he collected. Today it is still necessary to use the same methods to move governments and people: Peter Townsend's work (1957, 1965) carries on the same traditions of seeking reform by demonstrating the need for it.

In the USA a similar concern for the underprivileged was the impetus behind the growth of American sociology. The American Social Science Association which was the father of the American Sociological Society was founded out of a concern for the poor. The first president of the American Sociological Society, Lester Ward, said that 'the real object of science is to benefit man. A science which fails to do this, however agreeable its study, is lifeless' (quoted in Friedrichs, 1970, p. 172). Ward like many other early sociologists had connections with established religion: his grandfather was a clergyman as were Giddings and W. I. Thomas's fathers. Sumner, Henderson and Small were all clergymen while Ellsworth Faris had been a missionary. The first formal teaching of sociology was by a minister, C. R. Henderson and in 1885 out of eleven institutions teaching sociology in the USA five were theological seminaries. Sociology was practical Christianity. Moreover most of the early American sociologists were also from agrarian backgrounds. This may explain in part their concern with the effects of industrialisation. People with a concern for social welfare rather than for the scientific study of society also provided the finance for many early sociological studies. Shaw, for example, who developed the ecological survey, was a probation officer and received funds for his research from bodies such as the Chicago Women's Club who were concerned with the problems of delinquent boys. Shaw was not alone in his interest in social work. A survey of the members of the American Sociological Society in 1933 (Duncan and Duncan, 1933) found that most sociologists stated their primary interest to be social work.

This reform emphasis persisted in British social surveys longer than it did in the USA. Perhaps the opportunity that was available in Britain to use sociological research for political ends, its origins tracing back through Seebohm Rowntree (1871–1954) and Charles Booth (1840–1916) to the Reform Parliament of the early 1800s, meant that those engaged in social surveys became involved in politics rather than university life, thus diverting minds to administration rather than academic study. Whatever the reasons it was in America that the social survey developed beyond describing the poor and their housing. The development really came from the study of voting behaviour. The Gallup polls had produced a means of predicting election results and Lazarsfeld and his co-workers adopted these techniques in their study of voting, *The People's Choice* (1948), which looked at why people had voted, and in so doing made of the survey an *ex post factum* experiment, in which variables are controlled by holding them constant after the data have been collected by survey methods.

Observation and life histories

The urban poor who had been the focus of the social survey also formed the focus for the observation techniques of participant observation and life histories. The curiosity about the unusual and exotic in society led to the development of the methods of participant observation and the life history. The middle-class sociologists, particularly in Chicago in the early 1920s, found that there were all sorts of groups of people around them who had a completely alien life style from their own. Spurred on by Park, who was a professor at Chicago, they developed participant observation and life histories to study these people. The fact that Park had been a journalist may have been a contributory factor in the development of these techniques. The main factor however was undoubtedly that it was not possible to study these curious groups in any other way. Just as anthropologists were beginning to realise, following Malinowski's pioneer work, that to understand primitive societies meant living with them, so the sociologists at Chicago came to the same conclusion. There may even have been some anthropological influence; it is known that the works of Boas, an anthropologist, were recommended reading for Park's graduate students. A series of books emerged using the participant observation technique that have become sociological classics: Anderson's *The Hobo* (1923), Thrasher's *The Gang* (1927) and Zorbaugh's *The Gold Coast and the Slum* (1929).

Open to the sociologist, although not to the anthropologist, was the alternative technique in a literate society of obtaining written accounts of the groups they lived in, by members of the groups. This was usually approached by getting a member of a group to write his life history. This technique is perhaps best exemplified in Shaw's *The Jack-Roller* (1930). The curiosity about the unusual held by the researchers of the day can be seen in Burgess's recollections:

> I recall Nels Anderson telling me he was greatly bored by his landlady, in the roominghouse district where he was studying the homeless man, telling him her life history. I told him, 'Why, this is valuable, you must get it down on paper.' I still have this document; it is most revealing. Who becomes a roominghouse keeper? Who is the star boarder? How do you keep a roominghouse orderly against all the tendencies toward disorder in a roominghouse district? Out of his one document you get more insight into how life moves in the roominghouse area, and especially from the standpoint of the roominghouse keeper, than you do from a mountain of statistics that may be gathered (Burgess and Bogue 1964, p. 9).

The middle-class voyeurism that is part of this method is glaringly obvious. It has been said that anthropology can be defined as white men studying black men. What is not so often stated is that sociology, in its origins at least, contained a similar pattern of middle-class men studying working-class men. (This tendency to look down on those studied affects not only this research method but is a problem endemic in sociology. The attempt at detachment and the treatment of men's social life in terms of symbols may have a dehumanising effect. As Friedrichs (1970, p. 172) points out: 'Manipulating symbols of man rather than man himself may indeed be a greater actual threat to the traditional image of the humanity of man than any steps that have been taken to date to "control" him physically.')

Apart from a more rigorous realisation of the problems involved in participant observation there has been little development of this technique although there have been many stimulating examples of it, particularly in the works of Becker and Goffman. The life history, as a method, after a vigorous debate in 1945 between W.I. Thomas and Stouffer about its efficacy in opposition to attitude surveys has virtually disappeared as a sociological technique. Tony Parker's books (1969, 1970) still employ a variant of it, the tape-recorded interview, in the field of criminology but these are outside the mainstream of academic sociology.

Comparative method

The comparative method derives most directly from the Prophets of Paris. It was until 1918 the dominant method of sociology although after that date it suffered a rapid decline. Its decline was associated with the decline of its basic idea—progress, which after the carnage of the Great War no longer seemed such an inevitable social law. The idea that society was in a state of progress from previous more barbaric ages was in the nineteenth century a commonplace of philosophic thought that was rarely challenged. The confusion of technological with moral progress was a common error of that age, which still persists today, in spite of Nazi Germany. The discoveries of tribes in remote areas of the world who were technologically primitive led thinkers to take such people as evidencing earlier historical periods, living fossils. At the same time there did appear to be political and economic progress, if progress was defined as greater political freedom and more wealth, and it was so defined. Later in the nineteenth century the findings of geology, and Darwin's theory of evolution gave a boost to the idea of progress in sociology that served to support an already existing Social Darwinism developed by Spencer. The beginnings of the idea of progress in society are however to be found in the writings of Condorcet, Saint-Simon and Comte. Condorcet had argued for the idea of continuous progress and

17

Comte suggested that that progress was evidenced in three stages; the first stage was the 'theological', where supernatural beings were invoked to explain causes; the second was the 'metaphysical', where causes were sought in abstract forces; and the third was the 'positive' stage where no absolute causes were sought, only laws of coexistence and sequence. He held that deliberate intervention in evolution is limited because progress is determined by positive law (i.e. is inevitable) and all that men can do is to modify secondary forces and thus speed up change. The similarity of this argument to Marx's argument that the revolution of the proletariat was inevitable, yet men must bring it about, is striking. Marx also borrowed from Saint-Simon and his followers who had created utopian schemes for the new order that was about to dawn.

As well as the Marxian variant of the idea of progress there was also the school of thought that was known as Social Darwinism. The most famous exponent of this school was an Englishman, Herbert Spencer, who conceived of progress as an evolutionary process in which, to use a phrase he coined, 'the survival of the fittest' would produce the most effective social structures. Spencer dominated sociology in England and the USA at the beginning of the twentieth century, perhaps because his ideas fitted in so well with the laissez faire business ethic of that time. If progress was to be achieved, Spencer argued, then government should not interfere in the social world to alleviate poverty or for any other reason, for this was to interfere in the evolutionary process: a sentiment that businessmen were happy to endorse. Not all Social Darwinists shared Spencer's opinions on the inadvisability of interference. The American, Ward, argued that once men understood social phenomena they could interfere to accelerate progress.

The method used by all these theorists, Comte, Marx and Spencer, was that of comparing different historical periods and from this comparison deducing laws of historical development. The fact that from examination of the same history Marx could come to one conclusion and Spencer to its opposite suggested that the laws were more the product of the observer than the data. This was not realised at the time and only Weber was sufficiently historically sophisticated to realise that it was impossible to deduce laws from historically unique phenomena. There were not enough comparable cases. Weber's answer to the problem was to develop the concept of the 'ideal type'. This was an abstraction of the essence of a historical phenomenon which might not occur in pure form in any empirical situation. Using this Weber was able to study the ethic of protestantism and the practice of capitalism as ideal types and to relate them. Although the concept of ideal type has been extensively used in sociology it failed to solve the problem posed by the uniqueness of historical events.

The comparative method, because it cannot be scientific, since history lacks sufficient cases to enable comparisons to be done and patterns to be found, has not been developed. But it has not been entirely abandoned: Sorokin, Pareto and Eisenstadt have all produced works which, although not in fashion at the moment, are in the direct tradition of the comparative method. A variant of this method which attempts to trace trends in recent history in the hope of predicting the future has become very popular. Ogburn's (1934) mammoth study was the first of such attempts and recent works in the same vein has been done by Kahn (1967) and Meadows (1972).

Measurement and analysis

The origins of the concern with measurement lie in two features of nineteenth-century life. The first was the scientific spirit already discussed. Science to those in that time meant measurement. The quotation at the front of this chapter from the Statistical Society of London captures this measurement madness as does another quotation from the Royal Statistical Society *Annals* (1934):

> A letter was read from Mr Mackenzie, Secretary to the National Philanthropic Association, suggesting that an endeavour be made to discover the quantities of horse-dung deposited daily in the streets of the Metropolis, and Mr Fletcher was requested to reply thereto to the effect that the Council have not at their disposal any funds of the Statistical Society applicable to such an investigation as that which is proposed and they do not consider it advisable to

take the credit or responsibility of expending the Funds of others upon it; but that they will be very glad to receive any paper on the subject amongst those which are constantly being submitted to the Society and give to it the place in the Society's transactions and publications which its relative merits and importance may demand (pp. 31–3).

This concern with the collection of facts was not confined to England: an American Statistical Association was founded in 1839 on the same lines as the Royal Statistical Society. The other source of this desire for facts lay in the rise of the nation states. Kings had always been interested in the number of their subjects, so that they could tax them. This was the origin of the Domesday Book. With the rise of the nation states governments became interested in other aspects of citizens than their ability to pay taxes. Part of this interest may have stemmed from the rapidly changing nature of society, so that constant checks were needed to discover what was occurring. Certainly in England much of the impetus came from the Utilitarian philosophy developed by Bentham. He had suggested that it was possible to calculate the effects of laws using the 'felicific calculus' as a means of assessing happiness. Laws could then be passed to achieve 'the greatest happiness of the greatest number'.

The pseudocertainty of Bentham was modified by the Reformed Parliament of England in the 1840s, but it retained his emphasis on the need to know what social conditions existed before attempting to legislate about them. This parliament developed means of social investigation—the forerunner of the social survey—and of tabulating the data collected. The office of Registrar General was created to deal with the collection of social statistics. His first medical statistician, Dr William Farr, created a national register of deaths. He used this register to seek the causes of death: for 'diseases are more easily prevented than cured, and the first step to their prevention is the discovery of their existing causes' (see Newman, 1939, p. 17). He did this by determining the degree of variation by age, sex, district, social class and circumstances. Chadwick's similar work (1842) is well known. In the Census of 1841 professional interviewers were used. The factory inspection system was created and used such techniques as 'tabular forms' (i.e. questionnaires) to obtain a record of the number of children employed. In Belgium Quetelet was performing a similar function for the government there and becoming very involved in the question of how data was to be collected and analysed. His advice to statisticans is as apposite today as it was in 1846:

> The major dangers are
> 1. Having preconceived ideas about the final result
> 2. Disregarding figures which contradict the result one would like to see come about
> 3. Not fully enumerating all causes and attributing to a single cause the resultant of several causes
> 4. Comparing data which are not comparable (Trans. Wilkes, p. 313).

Like Farr he attempted to relate social phenomena to each other and was particularly concerned with the causes of crime. His arguments about crime foreshadow the type of argument used by Durkheim in his study of suicide. He suggested that the researcher must not look for one cause when studying the crime of a country. Intelligence, or rather the lack of it, had been suggested as a cause of crime. He said it probably was important but other factors were also important, and certain crimes call for high intelligence. It is thus mistaken to take lack of intelligence as a cause of crime, especially if the intelligence of a population is assessed by the number of children attending school without even considering what is taught in the schools. The opposite theme was even more ridiculous. This suggested that high intelligence was related to crime, stemming from the fact that in some places the number of crimes was proportional to the number of children in school. Quetelet pointed out that the proponents of this view failed to realise that a higher population and increased wealth explained a greater school population and also meant that there was more opportunity for crime. He also noted that criminal statistics were as much a product of law as morality—a change in law had often meant a reduced number of crimes recorded in the statistics.

The attempt to quantify social phenomena entered sociological thinking, rather than administrative thinking, with the work of Le Play. Le Play, a graduate of the Ecole Polytechnique and a mining engineer, in his travels in Europe sought a method of quantifying the social world he observed. He achieved this by concentrating on family budgets. Arguing that the family was the key element of any society he then went on to argue that an understanding of the family could be gained by looking at its pattern of income and expenditure. His own childhood in a peasant fishing village may have had some influence on this choice of subject. Whatever the origins of his interest he was one of the first to put forward a social theory and attempt to test it by measuring social phenomena. His theory, that the family was the key element in society and different families could be taken to represent different societies, was clearly inadequate, nonetheless his work was important in suggesting that the social world was open to measurement. The most important and original work concerned with testing theories by empirical data was that of Durkheim in his book *Suicide* (1897). As a detailed account of this work is given in chapter 6, a brief summary is all that is necessary at this point. Durkheim used official data on the incidence of suicide from several European countries to argue that suicide, a highly individual act, could not be explained by climate, biology or psychology but only by what he called 'social facts'. By showing how suicide varied in different religious, sex and age groups he suggested a theory of its origins that was solely sociological.

After Durkheim the development of sociological analysis and measurement, as with much of sociology, belongs to a history of sociology in the USA. There the techniques developed by Durkheim were extended by Woofter, Rice and Ogburn. The measurement of social class was developed. From social psychology came the whole field of attitude measurement. The social structure of small groups was measured, using sociometry. The use of documents received a new slant with the development of content analysis. Finally the goal of sociology as a predictive science was achieved in criminology, by Burgess, and the Gluecks. The pre-eminence of American sociology in empirical research was such that sociology became known as the 'American science'. The reasons for this pre-eminence have never been fully teased out. Her wealth, both in money and in terms of the number of sociologists she produced, certainly played some part in it. The influx of European intellectuals may have had the effect of continually revitalising empirical approaches. (Among those who originally came from Europe were Adorno, Mannheim, Lazarsfeld and Lewin.) The tradition of practicality—a concern with applied rather than pure research, which in sociology means empirical research rather than metatheory—may also have been a factor. All these factors may have been significant, the history is too recent and still continuing to be sure which, if any, was of paramount importance.

SUMMARY

Intellectuals in the nineteenth century, faced with a rapidly changing world, sought to understand and control that world by the development of a science of society. The method they chose for the scientific study of society consisted of a search for historical laws and became known as the comparative method. Later researchers used experiments in an attempt to be scientific. The desire to be scientific was not the only force motivating early sociologists. They were compassionate men, curious about the world around them. To satisfy their curiosity about the working classes they created the methods of participant observation and the life history. Out of their compassion for the working classes they created the method of the social survey, and methods of analysing data collected in surveys, so that they could place before governments irrefutable evidence of hardship. These four methods —comparative method, participant observation, the experiment and the survey—remain the major sociological methods today.

The experiment 2

Orne describes how he asked some acquaintances to do the experimenter a favour by performing five press-ups and how they asked in
amazement *why*? He asked another similar group of people to take
part in a short experiment involving doing five press-ups and they
asked simply *where*?

Bannister and Fransella (1971, p. 102)

The method of science is the 'experimental method'. It was
first clearly set out by John Stuart Mill. He was interested in the
different types of logical argument that could be used to test ideas.
One of these five types, the 'method of difference', exemplified the
experimental method. This consists of having two objects, fluids,
groups of people, which are exactly the same in all important
respects. Into one of the empirical configurations a new factor is
introduced. The change that occurs in that configuration—the
object explodes, the fluid changes colour, the group of people
becomes violent—is compared with the other configuration to
which the new factor has not been added. Any difference between
the two can be attributed to the factor. The empirical grouping
that is subject to the new factor is called the 'experimental group';
the one that is not subject to the new factor is called the 'control
group'.

The problems involved in this procedure are three: ensuring
the two empirical configurations are alike in all important respects;
arranging the two empirical configurations into an experimental
and a control group; and measuring the change that has taken
place.

The first of these problems, the difficulty of ensuring that the two groups are alike, is one that can never, even in the natural sciences, be fully solved. There may be differences between two chemical samples that are not detected by researchers in spite of all their attempts at purification. They can only say the two samples are alike when their instruments detect no difference between them, but this lack of difference may be due to the imperfection of their instruments or their theory rather than to any real similarity. This problem is acute in the social sciences in which there is no clear theoretical paradigm to guide researchers and help them decide what to ignore or try to control. The physicist studying electromagnetism knows he can ignore the colour of the plastic insulation on his wires. The sociologist, lacking as developed a theory as the physicist, is never sure whether to ignore the fact that one of his control group is attractive—that a girl may have got higher ratings as a teacher because of her attractiveness rather than her skill. It is impossible to control for all aspects and so scientists control those factors which they know are theoretically important—lacking a clear and undisputed theory the sociologist finds experimental control very difficult. There are two methods of ensuring the experimental and control groups are alike in social research. The first is the use of samples matched in terms of variables that are known to be theoretically important, e.g. social class, sex. (A variant of this is to look at individuals in a survey and match them afterwards by assigning symbols representing individuals to groups. This 'ex post facto experiment' is discussed in the next chapter.) The second is to randomly assign individuals to groups. In this way one assumes that all variables are randomly distributed in each group and therefore each group is alike. This method is attractive where one is not sure what the important variables are.

The second problem, of assigning people to two groups, is practical and ethical. If one assigns people to two groups, telling them that one is a control group, some may resent being manipulated and this may affect the result of the experiment. On the other hand if one assigns people to groups without telling them, one immediately meets the ethical problems involved in the manipulation of human beings. (The manipulation of symbols of people in an *ex post facto* experiment does not avoid this ethical problem. Treating human beings as symbols is itself dehumanising.)

The third problem above, concerning measurement, also presents acute difficulties in the social sciences. The lack of a theoretical paradigm makes it difficult to decide how and what one should measure, just as it made it difficult to decide which were the variables that had to be controlled to produce two groups that are alike. More important, measurement forces the sociologist to face one of the basic dilemmas of sociology. In the act of measuring, the sociologist changes what he measures. His presence, or the presence of his measuring instruments, changes the behaviour of those studied. The use of concealed instruments may avoid the problem in the short run, although raising ethical problems, but in the long run the knowledge gained by the sociologist becomes shared by others and may change their behaviour. This is a fundamental paradox that makes the social sciences different from the natural sciences.

The practical and ethical problems involved in social experiments are acute. The term experiment is here used in its natural science sense. There has of course been extensive use of 'the method of differences'. The *ex post facto* experiment of the survey, computer simulation of international conflicts, and the comparative method, which looks at historical events in this way, are all attempts to conduct experiments on large groups. In the strict natural science sense, then, it is not surprising that there have been no experiments on large groups of people. The practical problems of controlling variables would negate any such attempt even if ethical justification could be found for such experimentation. Most experiments have been on small groups of people within the sub-discipline of social psychology. The small numbers involved make it easier to control variables, theoretical explanations can be much more limited in scope and ethical problems are less acute, although no less important, when dealing with a few people rather than a society.

The development of the experimental method is therefore closely tied to the development of social psychology. This field of study, which draws on both psychology and sociology, did not emerge until the beginning of the twentieth century: sociologists during the nineteenth century were concerned with the search for historical laws or explanations of the structure of society, not the minutiae of social interaction, and psychology did not emerge as a discipline until the latter part of the nineteenth century. Social psychology received its impetus from two Americans: Charles Cooley and G. H. Mead. These men developed between them the conception of the individual as a product of social interaction in small groups: the infant through a process of perceiving other people's reaction to its actions, develops a conception of self. Without this process of 'socialisation', a word deriving from the works of Cooley and Mead, the infant would remain an animal, not a human being. (For a more detailed discussion of this fascinating topic see Sprott, 1952.) Cooley's work was published in 1909 and although Mead's work was not published until 1934 his development of Cooley's concepts had a profound effect upon sociology because all postgraduates in Chicago University sociology department were required to attend his lectures. As the majority of sociology post-graduates in the USA were trained in Chicago his lectures had a profound influence.

Independently of Mead, Elton Mayo and his associates in a piece of empirical research became aware of the fact that the group affected the individual. Their study has become a classic of sociology because not only did they realise that the group affected the behaviour of its members, they also realised that trying to control the variables that affected the group's behaviour, for experimental purposes, in itself introduced a new variable into the experiment. This effect, associated with trying to control people in an experiment, has been known as the 'Hawthorne effect' ever since, because their experiments took place in the Hawthorne works of the Western Electric Company. The study of the effect of the group upon the individual was taken further by Sherif in 1935. Sherif showed that in a situation to which no previous guidelines existed, individuals would modify their perceptions to fit in with other group members' perceptions.

The study of the effect of the group on the individual was but one strand of social psychology. Another line of social psychology research was concerned with the group itself. Moreno developed a technique of measuring the friendship patterns in groups which became very popular under the name of sociometry (discussed in chapter 6). Kurt Lewin and his associates and followers looked at groups analytically and, using experimental techniques, looked at the effect of different leadership styles and different communication patterns to name but two of the many variables they studied. More recently Bales has taken the study of groups farther by looking at the processes that take place in groups, using for this purpose an observation schedule that has been closely associated with the development of sociological theory. Often these developments in social psychology were also developments in the use of the experimental method and each of these studies will be looked at in turn to trace this development.

HAWTHORNE STUDIES

The title of this section, Hawthorne studies, was chosen because the research at the Hawthorne plant in the suburbs of Chicago consisted of a series of linked studies, not a single experiment. Before looking at the experimental section of the study, which was the first section, all the various studies will be described to place the experimental study in context. The first piece of research at the Hawthorne works was initiated by the management of the factory. They wanted to know the effect of lighting on industrial output. In 1924 they therefore started an experiment in which illumination levels in three departments of the factory were gradually raised. Finding no clear relationship between changes in illumination level and output they decided to modify their experimental procedure by the use of a control group. They therefore divided up workers to form groups of equal experience, gave one group constant illumination and the other variable illumination. In both groups output rose. The researchers concluded that they had not controlled their variable illumination level precisely enough and went on to exclude daylight. Once again the output of both the experimental and control groups rose. Finally the researchers took two girls and raised the lighting level until at a set point the level was not raised, but the girls were told it was being raised and saw an electrician change the bulbs. In fact he merely substituted bulbs of the same intensity. The girls commented favourably on the increase in illumination. The same procedure was followed with decreasing illumination. The girls' output remained fairly constant throughout the experiment.

From these results the research workers of the Hawthorne plant decided first that light was a minor factor in its effect on output, and second, that their experiments had been unsuccessful because they had not controlled all the other variables properly. They therefore decided to study a small group of workers to get greater control of the variables. To help them in this task they called in the Harvard Department of Industrial Research. The research supervision became a joint task shared by Roethlisberger and Mayo of Harvard, and Dickson, head of the 'Employee Relations Research Department' of the Western Electric Company. They set about their study of a 'relay assembly room' using experimental methods. This is the study which is of interest in the development of the experiment and is discussed in detail later. For the moment it is the conclusion of the experiment that is important. The researchers concluded that it was the attitudes of the employees rather than their physical environment that affected their output. Consequently they undertook a large-scale interviewing task in which they encouraged workers to talk about their work. The problems involved in coding all the data they collected led them incidentally to develop a form of content analysis (see chapter 6 on measurement and analysis). In their interviews a theme that kept recurring was that of 'rate-fixing', i.e. the practice of groups of employees agreeing that a certain rate of output was fair and then maintaining that rate, even when it would pay individual members of the group to turn out a higher rate. They decided to study this phenomenon and influenced by Lloyd Warner they elected to study it by observation. Warner, who had trained as an anthropologist at Chicago University, suggested a framework for their observation derived from anthropology. He suggested they look at the official, formal organisation of work and then look for an unofficial, informal organisation and seek the functions fulfilled by the latter. This anthropological approach was adopted in the study of the 'bank wiring room'. The depression led to redundancies and a cutback in funds for research so the research concluded, with the study of the bank wiring room, in 1932.

It was the first of the studies, the experimental study of the relay assembly room, that was important in the development of the experimental method. The stated intention of the researchers was to study the physiological factors associated with output, in particular the factors of fatigue and monotony. They therefore chose a repetitive job for the study: the assembly of a telephone relay which consisted of putting thirty-five parts together on a frame and securing them with four screws. They wanted to avoid the problems of non-cooperation which had arisen in some of the lighting experiments and therefore obtained volunteers for the experiment—six girls. These girls had their output of completed relays measured by an ingenious mechanical device. As each relay was completed the girls dropped it through a hatch in the bench, which closed an electric circuit which in turn activated a perforating device which pricked a hole in a roll of paper tape; the number of holes gave a record of each girl's output and the space between the holes gave a record of her pace of output. The girls were observed by a researcher who, to avoid the problem of non-cooperation mentioned above, tried to solve any difficulties they encountered. The girls had physical examinations, daily temperature and humidity readings were taken and the factory's records of wage payments (which were related to output) were also kept. Finally the girls were interviewed regularly, to find out their attitudes to the experimental changes in the work as they occurred.

Having set up the experimental situation and allowed a settling in period the researchers began to change some variables in the situation. First they experimented with various lengths and times for rest periods and observed the effect on output. Four different variations were tried. Secondly they changed the length of the working day. Six different variations were tried.

They found that hourly output generally increased over the two years of the experiment even though working conditions were often the same at different periods in the experiment. They tried to find an explanation of the increase using five hypotheses:

1. material conditions had improved;
2. fatigue was less because of better conditions in the rest room;
3. the work was less monotonous;
4. increased wage incentives raised output;
5. social factors were influencing output.

In a detailed examination of these propositions the researchers found that only the last hypothesis was confirmed. The researchers wanted willing and cooperative subjects who would respond to the different experimentally imposed conditions, uninfluenced by so-called 'psychological factors' (Roethlisberger and Dickson, 1939, p. 181). They therefore sought to control the attitudes of the workers:

> In order that the experiment would not be spoiled by varying attitudes on the part of the operators toward the experimental changes introduced, it was thought necessary to make certain that to every change each girl gave whole-hearted co-operation. To this end, then, the experimenters directed their efforts with the result that almost all the practices common to the shop were altered (*ibid*).

The consequence of their attempt to control was to introduce a new and powerful variable into the experimental situation. As they say of themselves as investigators:

> They were entertaining two incompatible points of view. On the one hand, they were trying to maintain a controlled experiment in which they could test for the effects of single variables while holding all other factors constant. On the other hand, they were trying to create a human situation which remained unaffected by their own activities. By Period XIII [the last period of the relay room research] it had become evident that in human situations not only was it practically impossible to keep all other factors constant, but trying to

do so in itself introduced the biggest change of all; in other words, the investigators had not been studying an ordinary shop situation but a socially contrived situation of their own making (*ibid*, p. 183).

This realisation, that the control of experiments in sociology introduces a new variable into the experiment, has become known as the 'Hawthorne effect' after this research. It has also become generalised to include all acts of measurement in the social world. It is worth pointing out that this was not its meaning for the Hawthorne researchers. They saw the effect as one associated with the control of variables in experiments, not the act of measurement. In fact in their study of the bank wiring room they used observers and say of them that 'they were not observing a situation of their own making. . . . This is not to say they had no influence on the situation. They probably did have, but it is very unlikely that the investigators were merely observing a situation of their own creation' (*ibid*, pp. 530–1).

The Hawthorne research was important for the development of the experimental method in sociology because it demonstrated clearly the effect that was later to be named after it—that attempting to control the variables in a human situation introduced a new variable into the situation. It was an important set of research studies also in the stimulation it gave to other researchers. For example it stimulated Lewin to look at authority in groups (a work which will be examined later); it stimulated the study of industrial organisations as a complex of formal and informal groupings in the work of Argyris (1965) and Gouldner (1954) and it led Dalton (1950) and Roy (1952) to look at informal group resistance to wage incentive systems. In general, it led to developments both in small group research and in industrial sociology and although it has been strongly criticised (see for example Landsberger, 1958) it remains an important sociological study.

SHERIF

Sherif's study, made in 1935, represents a considerable advance on the Hawthorne experiment in several ways. First, it is an extremely simple and elegant study. The experiment provided a crucial test of a major theoretical idea in a simple manner. This simplicity was achieved by Sherif's paring down of the theoretical problem into a set of simple propositions. It was also achieved because Sherif was able to test these propositions and control all extraneous variables. This control of variables was the second way in which Sherif's work advanced experimental study of human groups. The control was achieved by an innovation in the social sciences: the social science laboratory. These laboratories, which were in essence rooms set aside for social psychology experiments, were not so important in themselves as in the idea they expressed. Many key experimental studies have been conducted outside laboratories—the study of leadership undertaken by Lewin and his associates was one such (see later)—but the laboratory gave physical and symbolic life to the idea that human behaviour could be studied experimentally.

Sherif had studied the sociological writings on the variability of cultural norms and had become interested in how norms were arrived at and their consequences for an individual. From his sociological readings Sherif had drawn the idea that new norms arise in situations where people have no guidelines. He specifically mentions the works of Durkheim, Shaw and Thrasher as influencing his ideas. From his psychological readings, particularly the field of Gestalt psychology, he had taken the idea that well structured situations set limits to psychological structuring. He therefore looked for a way to present experimental subjects with an unstructured situation to see if they would create norms, what effect these norms would have on subsequent behaviour and what would be the range of these norms. As so often with good research work Sherif spent more time grappling with the theoretical problems than actually in experimentation: 'It took two-and-a-half years to formulate the experimental setup, although only about six months were needed for the experiments themselves' (Sherif, 1936a, p. viii).

The unstructured situation that Sherif found suitable for his theoretical problem was produced by placing a light source in a darkened room. In this situation a person placed in the room will, lacking a frame of reference to fix the light, perceive it as moving. This illusion of movement is known as the autokinetic effect and it was this effect that Sherif utilised. Because he had a sound- and light-proof room and because there was no real movement of the light point, Sherif was able to control his experiment and ensure that any perception of movement came solely from the experimental subjects. The experimental procedure was quite simple. A number of male undergraduates were taken into the room and asked to assess how far the light moved. Some were taken in individually. After many observations they were then put with others in the room and each asked to give their assessment of the movement of the light. Others were taken in with other undergraduates the first time they were exposed to the experiment. Whether taken in individually or as one of a number of undergraduates, the experimental subjects were asked to call out their judgment of movement. All subjects, after their experience with others in the room, were taken in again individually and asked to give their judgments. A comparison of their judgments of movement, which it must be emphasised was purely illusory, was then made. All individuals set up their own 'norm' of movement: for variation they set up a reference point to which all subsequent movement was compared, a subjective reference point to which they compared subjective movement. In the situations where individuals were in the room together with others their judgment of movement converged with that of the others. Those individuals who started off with others in the room showed much closer agreement than those who first went in by themselves. When individuals were taken in alone after being in a group, they saw the movement in terms of the norm set by the group. Sherif was thus able to demonstrate experimentally the development of norms in groups, a phenomenon that had been assumed but never proved before. This use of the experiment to test sociological theories by abstracting the variables implicit in those theories was to be the form that experimental studies were to take after Sherif.

The connection between theory and experimentation was developed with considerable success by Kurt Lewin and his associates. Lewin was trained in the physical sciences in Germany, later becoming a professor of psychology at Berlin. He fled from Nazi Germany to America, where his interest in the social aspects of behaviour, already apparent in his psychological writings, became dominant. One suspects that his approach to sociological problems may have been strongly influenced by his training in natural science. His theory was concerned with 'forces', a natural science concept, and he was a great believer in the experiment: 'I am persuaded that it is possible to undertake experiments in sociology which have as much right to be called scientific experiments as those in physics and chemistry' (Lewin, 1939, p. 21). His work, and that of his associates and students, did much to make sociological experiments acceptable as scientific.

It is not possible to look at all Lewin's work, so one well-known and important study has been singled out for analysis. This is the study of the effects of different types of leadership made in collaboration with Lippitt and White. Before looking at this study it is necessary to look in general at Lewin's theoretical approach because it was this approach that changed the focus of the study of small groups. Before Lewin's work small groups had been studied as causes of individual behaviour. Sherif's work is perhaps the best example of this. Sherif was interested in the individual and only became interested in the group as a factor affecting the individual's behaviour. After Lewin's work the focus of small group research shifted to become an interest in the group, its structure and behaviour: the group of itself became the subject of experiments.

Lewin called his theoretical approach 'field theory'. The individual *and* his environment were seen as an interrelated system called a 'life-space'. The individual's desire to release 'tensions' gave vitality to the 'life-space'. The life-space was conceived of as a mathematical 'field' and the tensions were seen as 'vectors' in that field. As well as the individual's tensions, Lewin also conceived the life-space to be occupied by 'induced forces'. These were derived from the group to which an individual belonged, or from some other source such as a powerful person. The details and terminology of the theory are not important (for their application to the experiment described here see Lewin, 1947). What was important was that it stressed that the total situation was the 'reality' for study. This meant that the focus was to be on the individual *and* the environment as a unit, not just on the individual and the way he was affected by the environment. It stressed the *present* situation as the object of study—the individual was not seen as a consistent entity entering different situations over time, but as just one aspect of one situation. An exaggeration of Lewin's point may make the argument clear: whereas for other psychologists the basic unit of study was the individual and they were concerned with the influences on the individual, for Lewin the basic unit was the situation (or 'life-space') and the individual existed only as one element in that situation; when the situation changed a different individual was involved, even if it was the same physical person. The result of this emphasis was a concern with groups in which the group was seen to be as 'real' as the individual. Lewin then was concerned to state the reality of what Durkheim called 'social facts'. He said:

> Logically, there is no reason to distinguish between the reality of a molecule, an atom, or an ion, or more generally between the reality of a whole or its parts. There is no more magic behind the fact that groups have properties of their own, which are different from the properties of their subgroups or their individual members, than behind the fact that molecules have properties, which are different from the properties of the atoms or ions of which they are composed (Lewin, 1947, p. 8).

The way to demonstrate this reality was the experiment: 'The taboo against believing in the existence of a social entity is probably most effectively broken by handling this entity experimentally' (*ibid.*, p. 9).

The experiment that Lewin undertook with Lippitt and White

demonstrates both his theoretical emphasis on the total situation rather than the individual in a situation, and also his concern with the technicalities involved in achieving experimental control of variables. (Accounts of this experiment are given in Pugh, 1971, Proshansky and Seidenberg, 1965, and Lewin 1947, as well as numerous other places.) Because he had a theory which specified which variables would be important he was able to identify, control, and measure them in the experimental situation. The control of the variables was achieved in four ways. First, the boys who were experimental subjects were allocated to four groups so that each group had a distribution of boys matched in terms of a whole series of variables. To achieve this matching, before the experimental period began, the investigators studied the school classes from which the boys were drawn in detail. They observed the children in the classroom and in the playground. They administered sociometric tests and used them to identify isolates, friendly boys and leaders. They asked the teachers to rate the boys in terms of their behaviour: whether they teased others, showed off, were obedient or not and how energetic each was. Finally they examined the school records for estimates of the intelligence, physique and social class background of the pupils. Secondly, having obtained matched groups on all these variables the investigators achieved control by exposing each group to different social climates sequentially. In this way each group acted as its own control. This was, you may remember, the only way the Hawthorne researchers had produced control groups. Thirdly, all groups met in the same room, thus keeping the surroundings constant. Fourthly, as far as possible, each group undertook the same set of activities. The object of the experiment was to study the effect, upon groups, of different leadership styles. To achieve this the four matched groups of schoolboys participated in 'club' activities, e.g. mask-making, soap carving. Each group had a leader for a period of seven weeks who used a particular leadership style. At the end of seven weeks the group was given a new leader who used a different style. Although each group never had the same person for a leader twice, each leader played at each style in different groups. In this way it was possible to show that it was the leadership style, rather than the individual, that was associated with certain types of behaviour among the club members. Four observers sat in the room behind low burlap screens in shadow. The boys were told at the beginning of the experiment that these were people interested in club activities. These observers kept accounts of the behaviour in the room in minute detail. They kept:

1. A quantitative running account of the social interactions of the five children and their leader, in terms of symbols for directive, compliant and objective (factminded) approaches and responses, including a category of purposeful refusal to respond to a social approach.

2. A minute-by-minute group-structure analysis giving a record of: activity sub-groupings, whether the activity goal of each sub-group was initiated by the leader or spontaneously formed by the children, and ratings on degree of unity of each sub-grouping.

3. An interpretive running account of significant member actions, and changes in dynamics of the group as a whole.

4. Continuous stenographic records of all conversations. (Lewin *et al*, in Pugh 1971, p. 233).

In addition to these observations an interpretive account of interclub relationships was kept, each leader wrote up what he had seen after each meeting, comments by guest observers were noted and films were taken of certain aspects of group life. This massive effort to observe all the actions of a group was not the end of the attempts by Lewin and his associates to ensure experimental control. The observers' observations were checked for reliability, i.e. the investigators saw if all the observers had put down similar accounts of actions they had all observed. These accounts were then 'coded', i.e. put into simple form for analysis, and the coding procedure was also checked for reliability by getting different people to code the same material. The accounts were coded to supply indices of group behaviour: degree of aggressiveness, frequency of recognition-seeking behaviour, proportion of organised to unorganised activity and so on. As well as the records obtained to place the boys into matched groups and the records of observations of group behaviour, the investigators collected another series of records about the boys by interviewing them after each seven-week period about their experiences in the club, interviewing their parents, talking to their teachers and administering Rorschach tests to each child.

The detail and rigour of this experiment far surpassed anything that had preceded it. It showed that social experiments on groups as such were possible. Because of the implications of its results, its concern with leadership styles, the results remain as a substantive contribution to sociology just as the method used was a substantive contribution. The detail of the experiment produced detailed results and it is not possible to report them all here, but a few are presented to give an impression of the work. The leadership styles that were adopted were authoritarian, democratic and laissez faire. What these terms meant, like everything else in this experiment, was closely specified by the investigators, but for an understanding of the results it is sufficient to say that the authoritarian leader determined all activity, the democratic leader left activities open to group discussion with guidance from the leader and the laissez faire leader gave the boys complete freedom. For purposes of example the results relating to agressive behaviour are presented (see Figure 1).

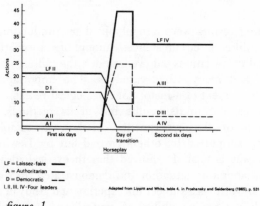

LF = Laissez-faire ━━━
A = Authoritarian ━━━
D = Democratic ━ ━
I, II, III, IV - Four leaders

Adapted from Lippitt and White, table 4, in Proshansky and Seidenberg (1965), p. 531

figure 1

39

The low aggression shown under authoritarian leadership is interesting as is the great increase in aggression in two groups upon their release from authoritarian leadership.

The researchers also used what they called 'test situations'. These were of three kinds: the leader left the room, he arrived late and a stranger entered the room when the leader was out and criticised the boys' work. As can be seen from the diagram below (Figure 2) the intrusion of a hostile stranger produced aggression.

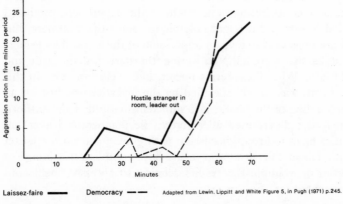

figure 2

Interesting results were also obtained on production rates of boys under different circumstances, amount of scapegoating, range of personality variations allowed under the different styles of leadership and many other variables. The importance of the study in the context of a history of sociological research methods lies, however, not in its results but in its methods. For the development of the experimental method in sociology this experiment, supported by others carried out by Lewin and his associates, was crucial. It showed that theoretical ideas can be tested in a laboratory situation and demonstrated the availability of the social world as a subject for experimental study in a manner that established the possibility of controlling the variables in a social ·experiment, just as it is possible to control variables in the physical sciences. It was a most important study.

BALES

Lewin may be said to have related theory and empirical research but this integration lay largely in the orientation the theory gave to the research: the emphasis on the situation rather than the individual. In the work of Bales a much closer integration between theory and research emerged. Like Lewin, Bales was interested in the situation and the acts that occurred in the situation rather than the individual. In this respect his work echoes Lewin's in its treatment of the individual as a participating actor in a unique situation rather than as an entity bringing previous experiences to the situation: 'This . . . actor stands behind the overt act, persists through it and ties the present act to acts which have gone before and to acts which are to come, but is nevertheless not identical with the more extended self seen as object by the actor' (Bales, 1951a, p. 43).

In practice Bales's experimental designs take this view to its logical conclusion. In his experiments the participants are brought together just for the purposes of the experiment and are identified by numbers. Their experiences outside the experimental room are specifically excluded from study. This contrasts sharply with the extensive attempts Lewin made to find out his experimental subjects' background and attitudes before and during the experiment. It is in his integration of theory and empirical research that Bales differs most sharply from any previous researcher. He differs because the categories he uses to study behaviour derive directly from theory.

The theory referred to is the 'action theory' developed by Talcott Parsons at Harvard. In conversations with Parsons, Bales adopted the idea that any social system is faced with six functional problems. These problems can be represented by twelve categories which can be used for observing behaviour:

The set of twelve categories (and the actual behaviour which is classified under them) are brought into working relation to other bodies of theory in terms of the frame of reference. The key assumption which provides this articulation is the notion that all organised and at least partially cooperative systems of human interaction, from the smallest to the most inclusive, and of whatever concrete variety, may be approached for scientific analysis by abstracting from the events which go on within them in such a way as to relate the consequences of these events to a set of concepts formulating what are hypothetically called 'functional problems of interaction systems.'

For purposes of the present set of categories we postulate six interlocking functional problems which are logically applicable to any concrete interaction system . . . problems of orientation, evaluation, control, decision, tension-management and integration (Bales, 1950, p. 43).

It must not be assumed that the construction of the twelve categories followed entirely logically from the theory. When Bales began his work he had many more than twelve categories for observation. He found however that observers could not cope with the large number of categories he presented them with and was forced to reduce the number. This was achieved by ignoring the social relationships among the experimental subjects and concentrating solely on their actions. In this way one category sufficed where three or more had existed before.

The application of the twelve observational categories took place in a social research laboratory. In Harvard this was a large room in which the experimental subjects sat, which contained a raised observation room. The observation room had one wall of one-way mirrors so that the observers could see out but the experimental subjects could not see in. In the room were microphones so that the observers could hear all conversations. The actual process of observation required training. Observations using Bales's categories are taken as near continuously as is humanly possible, which means about every three seconds. Observers have to be trained to see what action is occurring, classify it into one of the twelve categories and record that classification. As the observational categories are applicable to both verbal and non-verbal behaviour this is not an easy task. In addition, although each category is short, the duplications of it in terms of the theory need also to be grasped by the observer and all the empirical variations possible in a category have to be understood. (There are about two pages explaining each observational category in the training manual for observers.) To aid observers a moving paper tape, divided into twelve rows, to represent each category, continually passes in front of them, on which they record their observations in a simple code. Two observers record each experiment and to ensure reliability their paper tapes are compared at the end of the experiment. The observers listen to a recording of the experiment and rescore it. These rescored tapes are compared with the originals. Next a selected part of the experiment is rehashed with a third observer. Then three experienced observers are given copies of the tapes and listen to a recording of the experiment. When all this is completed the final account of the experiment is accepted as reliable.

The usefulness of the observational categories is that they are general enough to be applicable to all sorts of groups yet specific enough to relate directly to the actions of experimental subjects. Because of their usefulness in these respects the categories have been used in a very large number of experiments. This continuous use in different situations of the same categories for classifying behaviour, means that all the different studies can be compared, in itself a rare event in sociology. (This process is aided by the fact that each act is represented by an IBM punch-card on which the number of the person initiating the act, the number of the person receiving it and the category in which the act falls is recorded. Secondary analysis of other people's research is thus very simply achieved by re-running their cards on a punch-card machine.)

Comparisons of this nature can elicit results which are not inherent in the original research upon which the observations were made. In this way general statements about the structure of groups can be made with some confidence; Bales and others (1951b) analysed eighteen groups' interactions and were able to demonstrate that the people who initiate most acts also receive most acts, a finding not apparent in the original researches. The categories are also useful because observations are taken continuously, thus the process of interaction can be studied as well as the structure of the group. From the study of interaction it is possible to show that there is a pattern of interaction in most group meetings in the experimental situation: information giving decreases while suggestions and negative reactions increase, as time passes.

A short account of an experiment which used Bales's categories may illustrate their usefulness. For this purpose a study of leadership was chosen so that it could be compared with the work of Lewin discussed earlier in this chapter. The categories used are presented in Figure 3.

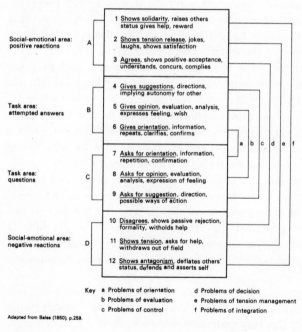

Social-emotional area: positive reactions — A
1 Shows solidarity, raises others status gives help, reward
2 Shows tension release, jokes, laughs, shows satisfaction
3 Agrees, shows positive acceptance, understands, concurs, complies

Task area: attempted answers — B
4 Gives suggestions, directions, implying autonomy for other
5 Gives opinion, evaluation, analysis, expresses feeling, wish
6 Gives orientation, information, repeats, clarifies, confirms

Task area: questions — C
7 Asks for orientation, information, repetition, confirmation
8 Asks for opinion, evaluation, analysis, expression of feeling
9 Asks for suggestion, direction, possible ways of action

Social-emotional area: negative reactions — D
10 Disagrees, shows passive rejection, formality, witholds help
11 Shows tension, asks for help, withdraws out of field
12 Shows antagonism, deflates others' status, defends and asserts self

a b c d e f

Key
a Problems of orientation
b Problems of evaluation
c Problems of control
d Problems of decision
e Problems of tension management
f Problems of integration

Adapted from Bales (1950), p.259.

figure 3

The study (reported in Madge, 1963, pp. 449–53) attempted to use the categories to look at two types of leadership. In Lewin's terms these were laissez-faire and democratic leadership. The same person played both roles. A look at the 'interaction profiles' of the groups concerned shows clearly that members spoke more under a laissez-faire leader and showed high agreement and high tension (Figure 4). Under a democratic leader the members spoke less,

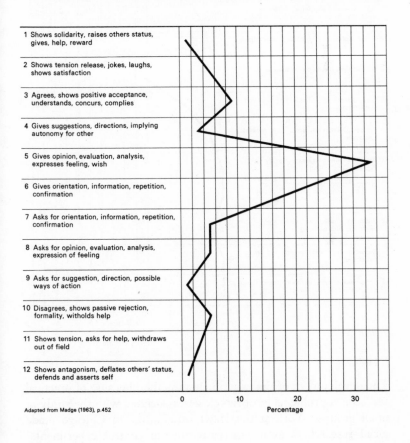

Adapted from Madge (1963), p.452

figure 4

were less likely to agree and showed greater tension release (Figure 5).

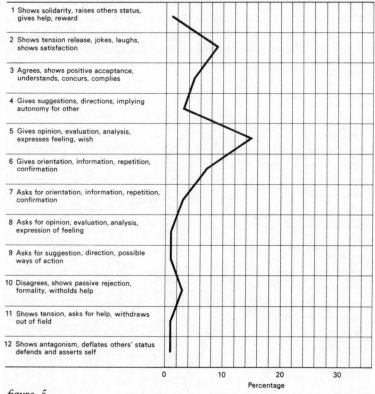

figure 5

SUMMARY

The development of the experimental method because of practical and ethical problems has been closely associated with the study of small groups. Work at the Hawthorne works in Chicago made social researchers aware that attempts to control experimental variables introduced a new variable into the situation: the social influence of the researchers themselves. The experiment was advanced further by Sherif, who was a pioneer in the use of social psychology laboratories and the use of the experiment to test significant theoretical ideas in sociology. The process of testing theoretical ideas was taken further by Lewin. Lewin also contributed to the development of experimental method by his insistence that it was possible to conduct social experiments and his demonstration of that possibility in experiments which had sophisticated methods of controlling variables. Lewin's work was seminal also for the study of small groups. Because of his theoretical orientation he turned the study of small groups away from a study of their influence upon individuals toward a study of groups as such. The study of groups was carried further by Bales who showed a similar rigour in his attempts to achieve reliability as Lewin and who, like Lewin, was interested in small groups as such. Bales went further than Lewin in the integration, in his work, of theory and the categories for empirical observations. Also he advanced the study of small groups because his categories allowed a study of process as well as structure.

The survey

The purpose of the study [of society] is twofold. First there is the purely scientific end of description, of classification and of investigation of causes. Secondly there is the utilitarian end of obtaining such knowledge of conditions and their relations, that we may be able to modify them with a view to constructing a society more in accordance with some ideal. Bowley (1915b, p. 7).

First the investigator knows what he wishes to discover. . . . If he is still within the realm of the "what" of life he may obtain satisfactory answers to his queries. If he enters upon the "why" and the "how" of life, which he must do if he is to learn anything about process as distinguished from status, he cannot rely upon simple answers to his categorical questions. The "yes-or-no", "black-or-white" view of life is not only a simplification but it is in reality a falsification.
Lindeman (1924 pp. 181–2) discussing the limitations of the survey.

The social survey grew out of a concern for the poor in the large city and a desire to understand and help those in poverty. Its methods were the methods developed by the nation state to enumerate its people: the painstaking accumulation of 'facts' to make 'statistics'. Charles Booth extended and broadened the survey so that it became more than an accumulation of facts. Paradoxically he broadened the method by limiting the area to which it applied. Before Booth's work most surveys were national censuses, or at least county censuses. Booth limited the survey to one place. More important, this place was an industrial city: London. This led him to several innovations that were to prove fruitful to sociology. First it led him into a concern with the spatial distribution of the 'fact' he was interested in, namely poverty. In an attempt to find some means of classifying his facts he turned to maps as a simple diagrammatic summary of the facts he was collecting. This use of maps formed the starting point for the field of urban ecology that was developed in Chicago and was to lead to the classic studies of Shaw and Thrasher in juvenile delinquency as well as many other studies of the spatial distribution of social phenomena. Secondly, he became concerned with the relationship between social class and social institutions in an area. This concern, coupled with the map-making, was the beginning of the field of study known as community studies: the study of the interrelationship of social phenomena in a small urban area which was developed by the Lynds and Lloyd Warner. Thirdly, Booth tried to relate the facts he had found, one to another, to determine causes, in particular the causes of poverty. This attempt to discover causes by the manipulation of survey data was to be developed to such an extent that Lazarsfeld's work on voting in America led to the survey being called 'an experiment after the fact', because the control of variables had become so sophisticated as to ape experimental control.

In Booth's work then can be perceived the first beginnings of urban ecology, community studies and techniques of analysing survey data that relate one 'fact' to another in the search for causes. More directly the extension of Booth's work by Bowley to five small towns was to lead to the development of the sampling techniques which play such a large part in surveys today. Each of these developments of the social survey will be examined in this chapter.

BOOTH'S SURVEYS

Charles Booth was not the first to use surveys—that technique of accumulating masses of tiny details to form one great picture. Before Booth, Engels (1845) had carried out a similar task in Manchester and Mayhew (1851) had carried out his extensive enquiries into the people of London. The state had conducted numerous surveys of health and welfare (see for example Farr's work, described by Newman, 1939). But Booth's contribution was unique: to make it he had to bring together the two existing strands. The first strand was that exemplified by Engels and Mayhew—the description of the poor; the second was that evidenced by the state—the quantification of social life. Booth quantified the idea of poverty. He did more than that. He related his measurements of poverty to other measures of income, occupation, residence and overcrowding, in an attempt to find causes; it is in this attempt that Booth's work was a great advance on previous work.

Booth was born in 1840, the second child of a prosperous corn merchant. He was born in Liverpool, into a world that is almost impossible to understand fully or even to imagine today. Liverpool was a town built on trade. Its leaders were merchants and ship-owners, men who had contact with all parts of the world. It was a port into which raw materials poured into Lancashire to be made into finished cotton cloth and industrial machinery for export from the same wharves. To facilitate this contact with its hinterland the railways had been developed and the first true passenger line in the world had been opened ten years before Booth's birth, between Liverpool and Manchester. In this bustling atmosphere Booth grew up, went to school and then entered apprenticeship as a clerk in a shipping line. After an interrupted grand tour of Europe, cut short by the death of a childhood sweetheart, he joined his brother in a business that took him to America for eighteen months. When he returned to open a branch of the business in Liverpool he also set up his own business: a shipping line. In this he played a large part in the development of steamships.

Booth's experience in business was to become important later when he developed his social survey. In the first place it gave him the money to finance his surveys. It has been estimated that they cost him £33,000, a figure which in 1972 would be equivalent to a quarter of a million pounds. Secondly his business experience led him to try to find all the facts before taking a decision and this may have influenced his attempts to find all the facts about poverty before seeking the means to alleviate it. Another influence on his desire to seek facts was undoubtedly his dabblings in Comtean positivism which during the middle of the nineteenth century was almost as much a religious sect as a scheme of understanding society. Although ultimately he abandoned the extreme rejection of religion implicit in positivism some of the ideas about the possibility of a science of society almost certainly stuck.

The seven years from 1866, when he had firmly established his shipping business, to 1873 when the wife he married in 1871 bore their first child, were years of strain for Booth. His business was demanding. He had estranged himself from his family by his espousal of positivism. He had attempted political action: the political organisation of workers, the establishment of a hall where they could be educated, and a proposal for universal secular education. All had failed. This political work, like his later social survey work, was done as an addition to his business commitments. An anecdote illustrates his capacity for work: 'His children recollect . . . that in order to put the time spent [commuting from London to home] to good use, he would perch a row of candle-ends along the carriage window-sill by which to read' (Simey and Simey, 1960, p. 98n). Although the strain of coping with a business, a child, political failure and continual self-doubt about his rejection of religion was to culminate in the first of a series of breakdowns in 1873, these seven years were also influential in forming the personality of the person who was to conduct the survey of the London poor. The businessman's concern with facts, the positivist's concern with facts, and the realisation that he could not achieve reform by political means must all have been influential in turning Booth's energies in 1886 to an attempt to find the causes of poverty by an extensive survey of London.

After his breakdown Booth retired to Europe for two years to rest. On his return in 1875, after recovery, he moved to London. In London he joined the Royal Statistical Society, a move no doubt influenced by his early interest in positivism. He produced for them an analysis of the 1881 census which gave him valuable experience in the handling of data, a realisation of the limitations of census data and useful contacts in the office of the Registrar

General. In London he also developed the habit of walking around the East End observing the people with a fascination that gave him a desire to understand their poverty.

The final impetus that led him to start the work for which he is now remembered came because H.M. Hyndman of the Social Democratic Federation had said 25 per cent of London workers were poor. Booth considered the figure grossly exaggerated and set out on work which he estimated would take him three years and prove Hyndman wrong. In fact it took sixteen years and showed Hyndman, far from exaggerating, had underestimated the numbers of poor: Booth's final figure for the poor was 30 per cent of the population.

Although I have referred so far to Booth's work in the singular he did in fact undertake three major surveys. The first and most important was a survey of poverty, its incidence and extent; the second was a survey of industry, and the last a survey of religion. Although his methods showed consistent improvement it is the poverty survey which remains the most important. The later surveys were refinements of the original conception. This he stated as follows:

> *General Aim*: To connect poverty and wellbeing with conditions of employment. *Incidentally*, to describe the industrial peculiarities of London (and of modern towns generally) both as to character of work, character of workers, and of the influences which act upon both. (quoted in Simey and Simey, 1960, p. 79).

To achieve this he developed both a measure of poverty and a means of discovering its incidence. The measure of poverty was based on income. (In his later Industry series he also measured poverty by overcrowding and compared the two sets of results. The measures of overcrowding were later used by Bowley.)

The poor were defined as 'those who have a sufficiently regular though bare income, such as 18/- to 21/- per week for a moderate family ... those whose means may be sufficient, but are barely sufficient, for decent independent life' (Booth, 1887, p. 339).

This was the first operational definition of a concept in social science, i.e. it gave a means whereby the truth or falsity of hypotheses about poverty could be tested. The means he used to find the incidence of poor was to utilise the school board visitors. As he said of these officials:

> [They] perform amongst them a house-to-house visitation; every house in every street is in their books, and details are given of every family with children of school age. They begin their scheduling two or three years before the children attain school age, and a record remains in their books of the children who have left school. The occupation of the head of the family is noted down. Most of the visitors have been working in the same district for several years, and thus have an extensive knowledge of the people. It is their business to re-schedule for the Board once a year, but intermediate revisions are made in addition, and it is their duty to make themselves acquainted so far as possible, with the newcomers into their districts. They are in daily contact with the people and have a very considerable knowledge of the parents of the school children, especially of the poorest among them, and of the conditions under which they live (Booth, Poverty series i. 5).

In addition he also used other officials to give him data: school boards, relieving officers, district superintendents and the police. He also set up cross-checks on his results by asking schoolteachers to assign children in their class to his categories of 'social situation'. Although his definition of poverty was made in terms of income, in reality the measurement of poverty relied upon the reports of the school board visitors and the subjective judgements of the schoolteachers.

Booth developed his list of classes in what would today be called a 'pilot study'. Before starting on his survey throughout London, he studied the East End using the same methods as he intended to use for the full survey and presented his results for criticism to the Royal Society. The major difference between the 'pilot' and the full survey was that the pilot survey had related poverty to employment for each family. The centre of analysis was therefore the *family*. This of course was consistent with his stated aims. When he came to undertake the full survey however he found the volume of data was too much to cope with adequately so he adopted the *street* as the basic unit. Booth saw this as regrettable and in that it did not allow him to relate income, employment and poverty for each family it was regrettable. It was however also the starting point for his map making that was to play such a prominent part in his study of religion and form the basis of urban ecology via American imitators of Booth's methods. The classes were defined in terms of income but because the assessment was made in terms of the judgment of the school visitors and Booth's staff they were also a measure of social position. The classification used and the percentage in each category are given below (Booth, Poverty series, i, 33, ii, 21):

A.	The lowest class of occasional labourers, loafers, and semi-criminals		0.9	in poverty
B.	Casual earners	'very poor'	7.5	30.7 per cent
C.	Intermittent earnings	'poor'	22.3	
D.	Small regular earnings			
E.	Regular standard earnings	comfortable working class	51.5	in comfort
F.	Higher class labour			69.3 per cent
G.	Lower middle class	middle class	17.8	
H.	Upper middle class			
	Total		100.0	

Because Booth had developed these categories for describing families they were not entirely appropriate for describing streets. Thus although these categories formed the basis for classifying streets they were modified to distinguish within each category. The categories for map-making were different also in that streets of mixed classes had to be indicated. The final categories he used in his maps (*ibid.*, ii, 40–1) are:

Black—The lowest grade (corresponding to Class A), inhabited principally by occasional labourers, loafers, and semi-criminals—the elements of disorder.
Dark Blue—Very poor (corresponding to Class B), inhabited principally by casual labourers and others living from hand to mouth.

Light Blue—Standard poverty (corresponding to Classes C and D) inhabited principally by those whose earnings are small . . . whether they are so because of irregularity of work (C) or because of a low rate of pay (D).

Purple—Mixed with poverty (usually C and D with E and F, but including Class B in many cases).

Pink—Working class comfort. (Corresponding to Classes E and F, but containing also a large proportion of the lower middle class of small tradesmen and Class G.) These people keep no servants.

Red—Well-to-do; inhabited by middle-class families who keep one or two servants.

Yellow—Wealthy; hardly found in East London and little found in South London; inhabited by families who keep three or more servants, and whose houses are rated at £100 or more.

In addition to these quantitative indices of social class, developed to distinguish between the poor and the comfortable, although used for more sophisticated purposes in the religion surveys, Booth and his assistants also walked in the streets and sometimes even lived in the areas they were studying, to gain greater insight into the people and areas that interested them. The result of these enquiries into poverty was summarised in a set of tables that are of vital importance in the development of sociology (see Table 1).

The importance of these tables is that for the first time in sociology a researcher had tested a hypothesis about social life by collecting facts. The hypothesis that had been tested was that of individual responsibility. Throughout the nineteenth century the commonly accepted belief was that poverty was caused by idleness. Men could by their own efforts pull themselves out of poverty. The explanations were individual not social. Being individual, men could be blamed not society. Booth showed for the first time, in a way that made it difficult to gainsay him, that the cause of poverty was social not individual. It was questions of circumstance or questions of employment not questions of habit. The social world was opened to study.

This was Booth's major contribution to sociology. It has been overshadowed to some extent by the more elegant exposition of

TABLE I Statistics of poverty : causes by degree of poverty

Analysis of causes of "great poverty" (classes A and B)

		Per cent		Per cent	
1. Loafers	60	–		4	Questions of employment
2. Casual work	697	43	878	55	
3. Irregular work, low pay	141	9			
4. Small profits	40	3			
5. Drink (husband, or both husband and wife)	152	9	231	14	Questions of habit
6. Drunken or thriftless wife	79	5			
7. Illness or infirmity	170	10	441	27	Questions of circumstance
8. Large family	124	8			
9. Illness or large family, combined with irregular work	147	9			
		–	1,610	100	

Analysis of causes of "poverty" (classes C and D)

		Per cent		Per cent	
1. Loafers	–	–		–	Questions of employment
2. Low pay (regular earnings)	503	20	1,668	68	
3. Irregular earnings	1,052	43			
4. Small profits	113	5			
5. Drink (husband, or both husband and wife)	167	7	322	13	Questions of habit
6. Drunken or thriftless wife	155	6			
7. Illness or infirmity	123	5	476	19	Questions of circumstance
8. Large family	223	9			
9. Illness or large family, combined with irregular work	130	5			
		–	2,466	100	

Source: Booth, Poverty series, i. 147.

Durkheim on suicide (1897) which makes the same point (see chapter 6). It was, however, Booth rather than Durkheim who brought home the point to the educated man. The latter author was not translated until 1933 and though some Chicago sociologists had read his work in the original it was Booth's influence rather than Durkheim's that led to the achievements of the Chicago school in America. This was not Booth's only achievement. He also demonstrated, which Durkheim did not, that it was possible to go out into the world and collect facts to test a thesis. He was the first empirical sociologist, with the possible exception of Le Play. Those continuing his line of work, Bowley, Jones and Rowntree, were the only empirical sociologists until the growth of sociology in America in the 1920s. These then were Booth's contributions to sociology: a realisation that social rather than individual explanations had to be sought for poverty and the idea that propositions could be tested by going out to collect facts. He also had a subtle influence on the development of sociology in ways that were mediated by others who probably did not realise their full debt to his work. Implicit in Booth's later work on industry, and more especially on religion, were two themes that were later to emerge as community studies and urban ecology.

The concept of community as it was later perceived by the Lynds, Warner and their precursors and successors was not a concept used by Booth. However a major theme of community studies was also prominent in Booth's work, particularly in his studies of religion. This was the interrelation of social class and social institution. Throughout his work there is the implicit understanding that each class occupied its own area, its own little network of streets, and within that area it had its own institutions and culture:

> Each district has its character—its peculiar flavour. One seems to be conscious of it in the streets. It may be in the faces of the people or what they carry—perhaps a reflexion is thrown in this way from the prevailing trades—as it may be the sounds one hears, or in the character of the buildings (*ibid.*, i. 66).

Of the religious institutions he says:

> The middle class has gone, replaced by a non-churchgoing working class ... The Nonconformists are not a whit more successful than the Church ... Several of the Chapels that prospered here 'while the shopkeepers still lived over their shops' [i.e. before the middle class left] ... have been entirely closed. Their place is taken by special missions, connected, in most cases, with an active church elsewhere. With these missions the regular working class will have nothing to do (Religious Influences i, 134).

The secular institutions, the shops, are also subject to a similar analysis:

> A poor neighbourhood is also stamped by its shops. Bird-fanciers are mostly to be found in the mixed streets which lie near black districts. Fried fish, and still more stewed eel shops commonly mark the vicinity of great poverty, and a catmeat shop is seldom far removed from it. The cats themselves may be taken as a last test (Poverty Series i, 183).

This relationship between class and institution shades imperceptibly into an account of the relationship between class, institution, behaviour and areal location—the field of ecology. Booth used maps not only to mark off different gradations of poverty and wealth in different colours but also to mark the positions of different institutions by small spot marks. These spot maps allowed him to note the differential distribution of different institutions. For example: 'It is noticeable how indigenous is the general shop to the more central poor districts of London. Although the "inner" ring has only a little over a third of the total population of the metropolis, it contains 58 per cent of the general shopkeepers' (Industry series iii, 251n).

More important, because his studies took over seventeen years to complete he was forced to take account of changes and sought to explain them in terms of 'the general law of successive migration'. He saw movement as going out from the centre, each district being invaded in turn by those poorer than its present inhabitants: 'The red and yellow classes ("well-to-do" and "wealthy") are leaving, and the streets which they occupied are becoming pink and pink barred; whilst the streets which were formerly pink turn to purple and purple to light blue' (Religious Influences i, 15). This was the same process of change as was observed by the Chicago ecologists and is an early attempt to give an ecological explanation. The part of Booth's work which most strikingly resembles and foreshadows the ecological school occurred however not in any of his three volumes on poverty, industry and religion but in his final volume that tried to draw together all the strands of his enquiries. In this volume he grouped his data into fifty districts and the districts were ranked in relation to their average per cent of poverty, per cent of crowding, birth rate, death rate and rate of early marriage. These ranked variables were related to social class by the use of a coloured map. The relationship of rates of behaviour to area was to be the key feature of the ecological school.

Summary of Booth's contribution
Booth never claimed the title of sociologist and yet he was one of the key figures in the development of its methods. He tried to fit his data into no grand theory of human nature and so was ignored by the sociologists of his day and is still underrated today because of his lack of theorising. Yet if one were to ask 'what do sociologists do?' rather than 'what concepts do they use?', no better example could be given than Booth's work. Sociologists have propositions about the causes of a phenomenon—poverty is due to individual failings or poverty is due to the structure of society. They define operationally the concepts used in their propositions—poverty is having less than 18 shillings a week. They go and collect facts to test those propositions—the social survey. All these Booth accomplished, many of them he was the first to accomplish, particularly the seeking out of facts and the construction of methods of collecting them. Booth however not only developed these aspects of sociological methods he also had features in his work which mediated through American imitators and the mind of Robert Park were to re-emerge as the distinct and

fruitful areas of sociology known as community studies and urban ecology.

TECHNICAL ADVANCES

Once Booth had pointed the way advances quickly followed. Rowntree (1901) used the new knowledge of calories to calculate exactly the food requirements of a family and hence defined a more exact poverty line. It was, incidentally, not much different from Booth's line. More important, the method of random sampling was developed by Bowley (1915a) in his surveys of 1912–14. His explanation of the reasoning behind random sampling is simple and is worth quoting:

> There is very little doubt that the households were so chosen as to make a fair and unbiassed sample of that part of the population that lives in private houses. For each town a list of all houses as given in a directory . . . was obtained, and without reference to anything except the accidental order . . . in the list, one entry in twenty was ticked. The buildings so marked, other than shops, institutions, factories, etc., formed the sample. Very strict instructions were given that no house which was occupied should be omitted, however difficult it was to get information. . . . The adequacy of a fair sample of one in twenty must now be considered. It is evident that averages based on one house in twenty in every street in a town must give a composite result that is closely related to a result based on complete information, and that there is no reason why any percentage or average obtained should be in excess rather than in defect. It is further evident that the larger the number taken in the sample the more accurate will be the picture, and that the more general features will be presented with less uncertainty than the less common. . . . Thus, if 800 houses are examined in a town containing 16,000 houses, and 10 per cent in the town are four-roomed, then 10 per cent of 800, i.e. 80, is the most probable number of four-roomed houses that will be found in the sample (though such exactness will not often be reached), and it is more likely that 75 or 85 will be found than 70 or 90 (pp. 178–80).

The importance of random sampling and other methods of sampling developed later is that they enable statements to be made about populations without having to interview or visit all the members of a population. Bowley was able to complete his study in two years, whereas Booth took seventeen years. The analysis of data was also speeded up by the invention of the punch card machine. Developed by Hollerith in the United States of America for the American census in 1890, this machine was the forerunner of the modern computer. Each unit of analysis in the survey, usually a person, has its responses converted into a series of holes on a card. The card has eighty columns and ten rows. Thus, for example, a person answering yes to the first question on a question-naire would have a hole punched in the first column of his card. If he had answered no, no hole would have been punched. Where a hole is punched an electric current can pass, and the machine thus sorts out cards into piles according to whether a current has passed or not, i.e. whether the respondents answered yes or no. In this way thousands of cards can be sorted quickly and easily and by rerunning cards that were all 'yes' on column one, with the machine set to sort out column two it is possible to obtain cross classifications. Very complicated analysis is therefore quickly and easily done on the machine and until the invention of the computer, which does the same job, such a machine was an essential feature of any large social survey.

THE CHICAGO SCHOOL

The social survey continued to develop with various techniques of sampling for the collection of data and more and more sophis-ticated means of analysing the data. I will return to the develop-ments in analysis later when discussing Lazarsfeld's work but now I want to look in detail at two developments of the survey that have already been mentioned: ecology and community studies. Both these fields, like much else in sociology, were developed at Chicago in the 1920s, although the first major study of a community was done by the Lynds, who were not trained at Chicago.

The University of Chicago was vitally important for the development of sociology because it was the growth point for a sociology that was aware of its methods. Surveys, social ecology, community studies, participant observation, life histories and social trend analysis, had all been used before they were used at Chicago in the decade 1920 to 1930, but their problems, their advantages and in some cases their very name were not seen until the Chicago sociologists developed them. It seems appropriate therefore to look at Chicago University and its sociology department before looking at its contribution to urban ecology and community studies. Much that is said here has relevance not only to these two fields but also to later chapters on participant observation, the comparative method and social psychology.

Chicago was a new university. It had been built in 1892 using funds from Nelson Rockefeller, the oil millionaire. It was unusual in several ways. First, it paid its staff twice the normal salary. Thus from the beginning it was able to attract staff who were already important men in their fields in other universities. It was also able to attract men from outside university life. It was unusual also in its system of teaching. It operated a four semester year, rather than the conventional two semester year. American universities, and today some British ones, like the New University of Ulster, and Stirling in Scotland, operate on the semester system. This involves taking a series of units of study for a set period known as a semester. At the end of that period one has completed a unit. By collecting 'credits' for 'units' a degree is eventually obtained by amassing sufficient unit credits. Chicago, with its four semesters, operated without a vacation ensuring full utilisation of buildings. However staff were only obliged to teach three semesters. They could, if they wished, teach four semesters and get extra pay or teach four semesters and only be paid for three. In the latter case this meant that in three years they were able to have a full year free of teaching duties on full salary. The flexibility of this system for researchers meant opportunities for research and scholarship that were not available elsewhere.

The sociology department was lucky enough to have a whole series of lecturers and graduate students who were to make important contributions to sociology. Part of this pre-eminence came from the lack of any university sociology departments elsewhere. Only Columbia had a similar opportunity and failed to take it. Much must be attributed however to the men who taught and studied at Chicago. Among those connected with Chicago were Herbert Blumler, E. W. Burgess, Everett Hughes, A. W. Kornhauser, W. F. Ogburn, R. E. Park, R. Redfield, Clifford Shaw, Samuel Stouffer, L. L. Thurstone, W. L. Warner, L. Wirth, Edward Shils, A. K. Loumis, H. D. Laswell, A. R. Radcliffe-Brown, E. H. Sutherland, P. G. Cressey, R. E. L. Faris, E. F. Frazier, A. R. Lindesmith, C. S. Newcomb, W. C. Reckless, Nels Anderson, Willard Waller, H. Zorbaugh, Howard Becker, E. S. Bogardus, G. H. Mead and A. W. Small, all names that are familiar to those acquainted with sociological writings and all taught, were taught, or did research at Chicago. The two that must be singled out here are E. W. Burgess and R. E. Park for it was from these two men and their students that urban ecology and community studies developed. They were also responsible for students who developed participant observation and social psychology but these will be dealt with in later chapters. Also dealt with in a later chapter will be the contribution of Ogburn both to social trends and through his students to the development of attitude surveys.

SOCIAL ECOLOGY

The best account of the beginnings of social ecology is given by E. W. Burgess who was, with Park, an exponent of it as a research method:

> What were the points of view and the methods of research with which we began our studies? We assumed that the city had a characteristic organization and way of life that differentiated it from rural communities. Like rural communities, however, it was composed of natural areas, each having a particular function in the whole economy and life of the city, each area having its distinctive institutions, groups, and personalities. Often there were wide differences between communities which were very sharply demarcated.

We early decided that the natural areas could be significantly studied in two aspects:

First, their *spatial pattern*: the topography of the local community; the physical arrangements not only of the landscape but of the structures which man had constructed that sheltered the inhabitants and provided places of work and of play.

Second, their *cultural life*: their modes of living, customs, and standards. Now the first of these aspects, the spatial aspect, gave rise to ecological studies; all that could be mapped; the distribution, physical structures, institutions, groups, and individuals over an area (Burgess and Bogue, 1964 p. 7).

As Burgess says, recognition of spatial pattern was the beginning of urban ecology. The examination of cultural life, although it began in the same stream of research and thought, branched out to form the distinct field of community studies. The assumptions that Burgess refers to do not seem very revolutionary today but they were so when they were first put forward. The city was seen as an amorphous mass and the idea that there might be 'villages' within it, later called 'natural areas', was startling. The idea had come from two sources. Park with his journalistic background and, like Booth, his habit of wandering around the city must have had such a concept in his mind for many years. His important article, 'The City: suggestions for the investigation of human behaviour in an urban environment' which was published in 1915 contains allusions to such an idea with his suggestion that study be focused on the neighbourhood and that more should be known about segregated areas of the city—those areas that were later to be known as ghettos. Incidentally, he may have got the idea from reading Booth's work to which he refers in his article on 'The city as a social laboratory' (1929) as a precursor of community studies. He was often unaware of the sources of his ideas. Everett Hughes in a letter to Faris said of Park: 'He often did not know where he had got something. He never presented an idea until it had gone through the crucible of his own mind, and when it came out, he often did not know its source. He often asked me . . . where he had probably got an idea' (in Faris, 1967, p. 6n).

The other source was the work of Burgess and his students who had inherited a course on 'social pathology', i.e. social problems, from Henderson. Burgess had had experience in mapping data in his previous post where he had conducted a community study of Lawrence, Kansas, and had noted different delinquency rates in different areas. He continued this interest in the course he set up:

> I had students in my course on Social Pathology making maps of all types of social problems for which we could get data. From this began to emerge the realization that there was a definite pattern and structure to the city, and that many types of social problems were correlated with each other (Burgess and Bogue, 1964, pp. 3–4).

Park was quick to recognise the value of these maps and began a course with Burgess, called Field Studies. (This course was equally important in the development of community studies.) Because much of the data was easily available in other people's records this field showed a very rapid growth. Its growth was stimulated in 1923 when the department received a grant of $25,000 and set up the Local Community Research Committee. The University gained the grant because it already had an impressive record of research: Nels Anderson's *The Hobo* (1923) had been published and Thrasher had already started his study of gangs. The Committee decided that they needed a social research base map upon which to place data. This was an important step forward for ecology for:

> The value of this social research base map at once became evident. In plotting cases of poverty or family desertion or juvenile delin-quency, it was now perceived, as it had not been before, why certain strips of territory had no cases: there was no population there, as a result of their use for railroad lines or yards, or industry or commerce. Other districts had large areas of vacant property awaiting residential or industrial development. Often it was possible by this map to form hypotheses to explain the distribution of the phenomena plotted upon it. A uniform base map of this kind made feasible comparisons of a series of maps exhibiting different types of data. It was clear that the social research base map was one way, and a strikingly graphic way, of assembling and exhibiting basic social data. The

Committee solved the problem of exhibiting these maps so that they might readily be compared, by securing a large map hanger of a size adapted for the social research base maps with space for the display of forty maps. The map exhibit room soon became a mecca for class and conference groups as well as for research students, social workers, and visitors interested in examining and studying the basic social data which they presented (Burgess, in Smith and White, 1929, p. 57).

The importance of the ecological approach for sociology was that it restated once again that social phenomena had to be explained in social terms, not individual terms. Booth had shown that the causes of poverty were to be found in society not the individual. The Chicago sociologists showed this for a whole series of social problems: crime, mental and physical disease, prostitution, etc. They demonstrated this by showing that it was the place not the people who were associated with these problems. Problem areas remained problem areas when their population changed. These 'areas of disorganisation' absorbed successive waves of immigrants and each year their rates of social problems remained high. When the immigrants moved out to the suburbs the rate of social problems in the suburbs remained low. It was the disorganised social life of the area, not the people in it, which led to social problems. This was the contribution of urban ecology.

Three research workers developed this concept: Thrasher, Zorbaugh and Shaw. Each of these may be said to have brought out in greater detail and given empirical evidence for, theoretical concepts developed by Park and Burgess. Burgess had suggested that the city could be seen as a series of concentric rings—the central business area, then the industrial area and ultimately the residential area. Between the industrial area and the residential area he perceived 'a zone of transition' where there was cheap housing. The housing was cheap because it was next to factories and warehouses, and owners anticipating selling it to industries were not willing to effect repairs. This zone of transition was the focus of Thrasher's work. Park had suggested that in the city there were natural areas, and his is the best definition of the concept:

> A region is called "a natural area" because it comes into existence without design, and performs a function, though the function, as in the case of the slum, may be contrary to anybody's desires. It is a natural area because it has a natural history. The existence of these natural areas, each with its characteristic function, is some indication of the sort of thing the city turns out upon analysis to be—not as has been suggested earlier, an artifact merely, but in some sense, and to some degree, an organism.
>
> The city is, in fact, a constellation of natural areas, each with its own characteristic milieu, and each performing its specific function in the urban economy as a whole (Park, in Smith and White, 1929, p. 9).

This idea was recurrent in Park's work, though not thus clearly stated until 1929 after the completion of Zorbaugh's work, in which it was demonstrated and developed. Burgess had further suggested a 'law of succession' which was exactly the same as Booth's 'law of successive migration' and postulated that cities grew from the centre and that areas successively succumbed to an influx of poorer residents. Shaw's contribution was to show how this was related to a gradation of social problems, with central areas having the highest rates and a declining gradient of problems into the suburbs.

Thrasher

Thrasher was interested in the gangs of young people who lived in Chicago. Anderson (1923) in his study of the hobo had already shown that particular social groups occupied the slums. Thrasher's contribution was to make this point in a more rigorous manner with regard to gangs of juveniles. He counted 1,313 gangs in Chicago and marked their location on a map of that city. By today's standards his reporting of his methods is sadly deficient. He does not explain how he defined a gang for the purposes of his count nor does he explain how he located their position on the map. In spite of this lack there seems little doubt that his work was a great advance on previous work in its use of mapping and statistics. He not only gave the location of the gangs but also tabulated the number of members in gangs, the age range of gang members, and the ethnic composition of gangs. His work was to be a source of inspiration for later students of criminality in its study of the culture patterns of gangs (called the subculture of delinquency by later writers), gang leadership, and the internal social organisation of gangs. Its interest here lies however in its contribution to ecology.

Burgess had postulated a zone of transition around the central business area. Anderson's work was the only previous work in this field and had been very much a classic participant observation study. Although Thrasher (1963) used participant observation he also used the more quantitative mapping methods that were then being developed at Chicago. Using these methods he was able to demonstrate that juvenile gangs were a feature of the 'zone of transition' (see figure 6):

> The gang is almost invariably characteristic of regions that are interstitial to the more settled, more stable, and better organised portions of the city. The central tripartite empire of the gang occupies what is often called 'the poverty belt'—a region characterized by deteriorating neighborhoods, shifting populations, and the mobility and disorganization of the slum. Abandoned by those seeking homes in the better residential districts, encroached upon by business and industry, this zone is a distinctly interstitial phase of the city's growth. It is to a large extent isolated from the wider culture of the larger community by the processes of competition and conflict which have resulted in the selection of its population. Gangland is a phenomenon of human ecology (p. 20).

With Thrasher's work the theoretical conceptions of Burgess about concentric rings were shown to have an empirical reality, in Chicago at least, and a reality that was important to practical reformers. This was important to Thrasher who was, like Shaw, not an ivory tower academic. He was concerned with prevention as well as description and uses the concluding two chapters of his book to discuss means of 'attacking the problem' and 'crime prevention', suggesting a concentration of resources on the task of reorganising the community in the zone of transition rather than trying to reform individuals or groups. Reform, as it had been for Booth, was still a strong element in the survey method and as with Booth research had demonstrated a need for reform of the social structure rather than reform of the individual.

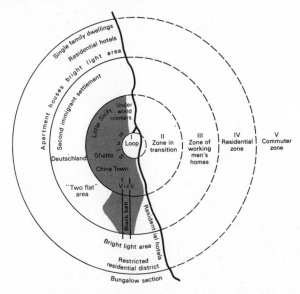

figure 6 The Place of Chicago's Gangland in the Urban Ecology The shaded portion indicates the approximate location of the central empire of gangland.

Zorbaugh

Thrasher's work had been published in 1927. By the time of its publication the ecological approach was firmly established in the Chicago sociology department. Mowrer's doctorate research, presented in 1924 and published in 1927 as *Family Disorganisation*, was concerned with the ecological distribution of different types of families in different areas of the city. In 1926 Ruth Cavan presented her doctorate on the ecological distribution of suicide in Chicago, published as *Suicide* in 1928, and Reckless had produced a doctorate, later published as *Vice in Chicago* (1933), which related prostitution to the ecology of the city in 1925. In this setting Zorbaugh, encouraged by Park, began his work on *The Gold Coast and the Slum* which was published in 1929.

Zorbaugh was fascinated by the contrast between two areas in the city—the 'Gold Coast' and the 'Slum'. The 'Gold Coast' was an area of apartments along the shore of Lake Michigan which was occupied by the social elite of Chicago. Immediately behind this area was an area of lodging houses and bedsitters:

> At the corner of Division Street and the Lake Shore Drive stands a tall apartment building in which seventeen-room apartments rent at one thousand dollars a month. One mile west, near Division Street and the river, Italian families are living in squalid basement rooms for which they pay six dollars a month. The greatest wealth in Chicago is concentrated along the Lake Shore Drive, in what is called the 'Gold Coast'. Almost at its back door, in 'Little Hell', is the greatest concentration of poverty in Chicago. Respectability, it would seem, is measured in rentals and land values! (Zorbaugh, 1929, p. 5).

In his attempt to describe the contrast between these two areas Zorbaugh looked at and mapped a whole series of indexes, e.g. the addresses of people in the *Social Register* (a local Who's Who), the addresses of suicides, the addresses of those arrested by the police in a raid on a night club, the incidence of crime, the addresses of business men's associations and so on. In this way he built up a picture of different subcultural areas in the city:

> One has a sense of distance as between the Gold Coast and Little Hell—distance that is not geographical but social. There are distances of language and custom. There are distances represented by wealth and the lustre it adds to human existence. There are distances of horizon—the Gold Coast living throughout the world while Little Hell is still only slowly emerging out of its old Sicilian villages. There are distances represented by the Gold Coast's absorbing professional interests. It is one world that revolves about the Lake Shore Drive, with its mansions, clubs, and motors, its benefits and assemblies. It is another world that revolves about the Dill Pickle Club, the soap boxes of Washington Square, or the shop of Romano the Barber. And each little world is absorbed in its own affairs (*ibid.*, p. 13).

Ecology had shown that there were different spatial patterns to social behaviour in the city. What Zorbaugh accomplished was the demonstration of the meaning of that differential distribution in terms of different subcultures. Before his work the concept of natural area was implicit in the ecological approach. After his work it became explicit. It is I think no accident that the first formal statement of the concept of natural area was made in 1929 by Park, the same year Zorbaugh's book was published for which Park wrote a preface.

Shaw

Shaw while a graduate student at Chicago had taken a job as a probation officer to work his way through college. In this job he was moved to different areas of Chicago and this may have given him his first ideas about the differing rates of delinquency in different areas. These ideas must have received theoretical under-pinning in his graduate studies. One idea that we know came from his studies which was to prove so valuable was that of 'gradient'. Shaw, like other graduate students at Chicago, was encouraged to read widely and explore areas outside his own subject. In one of these explorations he attended a biological lecture on ecology and there picked up the idea of 'gradient'. This was simply the pro-position that in an ecological area, the incidence of certain plants was greater in the centre, gradually decreasing toward the outside of the area. Shaw took this idea and applied it to social life, relating it to the concentric ring hypothesis of Burgess.

Working with McKay, another former Chicago graduate student, at Illinois, Shaw calculated delinquency rates by first finding the residence of boys convicted of crime. He then divided the number of juvenile criminals in an area by the number of boys in that area of juvenile court age. Having mapped these rates (see Fig. 7) it became apparent that they declined as one moved away from the centre of the city. In this way Shaw and McKay developed the concept of succession beyond the original formulation of Burgess.

This was not the end of the contribution made by Shaw to

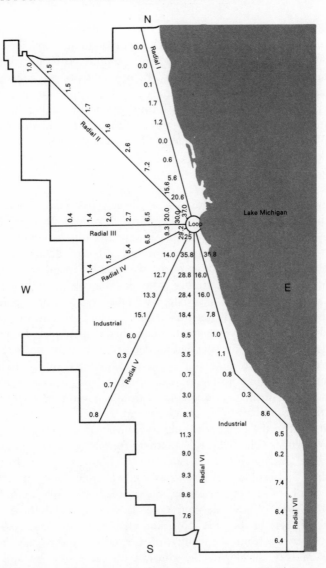

figure 7   Rate of Male Juvenile Delinquency by Square-Mile Areas along Lines Radiating from Loop.

urban ecology. Over a series of years and in a number of cities Shaw and McKay replicated their findings. This demonstrated that Burgess's model was applicable not only to Chicago but to other cities as well, a point which had been doubted by other sociologists. In doing this study they raised Burgess's conception from its local context and made of it, particularly in the work of McKay, a general theory of urban growth. In their research, by the sophisticated use of correlations, they also hammered home the idea that juvenile delinquency was associated with the social disorganisation of particular areas. Taking all the various theories to explain delinquency they created operational measures of each theory and correlated them both with delinquency and with each other. The result was to show that population change, bad housing, poverty, foreign born and Negro populations, tuberculosis, adult crime and mental disorders were all correlated with juvenile delinquency and each other. They argued therefore that because all these variables *inter*correlated then there must be some general factor related to them all. This they claimed was the social disorganisation of the area of transition. Acting upon this finding they attempted, like Thrasher, to create communities in the zone of transition. The Comtean positivists with their penchant for social engineering would have been delighted. Unfortunately they were unsuccessful but their research remains as a landmark in the history of the development of urban ecology and the social survey.

The contribution of ecology

Although ecology today seems to be the prerogative of geographers rather than sociologists it was important in the development of the social survey. It emphasised once again that social phenomena —vagrancy, suicide, crime, disease—had to be explained in social rather than individual terms. It was also important in that it was analytic. It concentrated on a particular variable and sought to show the relationship of this variable to other variables. This concentration of vision, by the ecological paradigm, resulted in the intensive analysis of specific topics and deep insights in a limited field, both the marks of a science.

COMMUNITY STUDIES

Community is a key concept in sociology, it seems therefore surprising that as a discrete area of study the study of the community should have such a late growth. The impetus for its growth came from two areas. The first was the survey movement, particularly the ecological school, discussed above. The other area was the field of anthropology. Community studies were in their inception, and have remained since, an attempt to apply the anthropological perspective to modern industrial society. Just as the anthropologist tries to explain the whole society he studies, so the student of a community tries to understand the whole community. To this end he uses survey methods. Community studies then are unlike the previous research methods which have been discussed. Like the comparative method, which will be discussed later, the stress is on the unique rather than the recurrent. The focus of a community study is on a unique community, and its methods are developed so that one community can be understood. In so doing it may find recurrent patterns in that community, but the understanding of the unique community is its goal. The experiment and the social survey are analytical methods concerned with the distribution of variables, be it normative compliance or poverty; the community study is not analytic in this sense. Its concern is with the unique, although proponents for the method point out that by the collection of studies of unique communities general patterns can be discerned. Frankenberg's work (1966) is a good example of this technique.

The social survey origins of community studies are much the same as the origins of urban ecology. Charles Booth's work was an obvious influence. In the United States, where community studies were developed in the 1930s, this influence was indirectly felt through the work of the Russell Sage Foundation. This was the body which financed the Department of Social Investigation of the Chicago School of Civics and Philanthropy. The work produced by this department was well known to Park and must have given him many of his ideas which were later to lead to the work of Zorbaugh (1929), Anderson (1923) and Wirth (1928) on urban communities.

The work of these three raised community study above the purely descriptive map-making level of the type carried out by such bodies as the Women's City and County Club of New York (cited in Colcord 1939, p. 18). These were studies of areas of a city, and although the concept of natural area enabled them to treat these areas as urban villages they would have been the first to admit that they were not studying a whole community but only aspects of it. The sheer size of Chicago may have been a contributing factor in the analytic approach that was developed there. Finding themselves, because of the magnitude of the city, unable to study it all, they were forced to look analytically at aspects of it.

A small town could be studied as a whole; a complex interrelated unit. The intellectual impetus that inspired the Lynds, and later Warner, to attempt to do just this came from anthropology. Durkheim in his study of religion (1912) had suggested that religion could be explained not by its historical origins but by the function it performed in society. This idea of seeking the function of an institution in relation to the whole society was taken up by anthropologists such as Malinowski and Radcliffe-Brown (the latter, incidentally, had studied in Chicago in the early 1930s). It was used as a sociological concept by the Lynds in their study of 'Middletown' (1929): 'the following pages aim to present a dynamic functional study of the contemporary life of this specific American community' (p. 6), and Wissler in his introduction points to the anthropological basis of this approach:

> So this volume needs no defence; it is put forth for what it is, a pioneer attempt to deal with a sample American community after the manner of social anthropology. To most people, anthropology is a mass of curious information about savages, and this is so far true, in that most of its observations are on the less civilized. What is not realised is that anthropology deals with the communities of

mankind, takes the community, or tribe, as the biological and social unit, and in its studies seeks to arrive at a perspective of society by comparing and contrasting these communities; and whatever may be the deficiencies of anthropology, it achieves a large measure of objectivity, because anthropologists are by the nature of the case "outsiders". To study ourselves as through the eye of an outsider is the basic difficulty in social science, and may be insurmountable, but the authors of this volume have made a serious attempt, by approaching an American community as an anthropologist does a primitive tribe. It is in this that the contribution lies, an experiment not only in method, but in a new field, the social anthropology of contemporary life (p. vi).

It was an idea that was to become a major sociological theory.

The Lynds

Robert Lynd, unlike most of the other American sociologists mentioned in this chapter and in this book, did not study at Chicago. He intended to be a minister and had studied at a theological seminary, after graduating from Princeton with an arts degree, and serving in the army during the Great War. In the early 1920s he became director of the Small City Study which was financed by the Institute of Social and Religious Research. The original intention of those who financed the study was that it would be a study of religious practice in a small American town. However Lynd, who was to direct the study, was influenced by Clark Wissler, an anthropologist at the American Museum of Natural History. Wissler, who wrote the foreword for the book on Middletown, introduced Lynd to the idea that an understanding of religion and religious practice required an understanding of a complete society in all its aspects. This, as pointed out above, was the functional approach in anthropology. Lynd decided to use it in his study.

The Lynds chose Muncie, Indiana, as a representative community for their study. It was small enough for all aspects of life to be covered, it was not a satellite of another town, it was industrial, it was growing and it had no large ethnic minorities. It was in fact a typical mid-west American town, celebrated in fiction from the works of Sinclair Lewis to the Peyton Place television series. Their theoretical approach, if it can be given that grand title, was to look at the activities of the town in terms of six categories of social life developed by the anthropologist Rivers. These categories form the chapter headings of their book and were: getting a living, making a home, training the young, using leisure, engaging in religious practices and engaging in community activities. Their methods showed no great originality. They used participant observation, documentary analysis, an examination of local authority statistics, formal and informal interviews and questionnaires. Their sampling method for obtaining their interviews was interesting because they used quota sampling, i.e. they chose their respondents to be typical of the town by looking at the wives of workers in the three main factories, ensuring that they interviewed people from different areas of the city and excluded families without schoolchildren or families with only one parent. Their cavalier method of obtaining replacement respondents for the sample by ringing the doorbells of other houses nearby contrasts sharply with Bowley's (1915a) research in which 'very strict instructions were given that no house which was occupied should be omitted, however difficult it was to get information' (p. 178).

Their analysis of documents is also interesting, because in their examination of the local newspapers and school magazines they counted the number of lines and the number of inches allocated to different categories of news at different times. In this way they were able to demonstrate the increasing importance of extra-curricular activities in the American school by showing the greater space allocated to them in the 'annuals' (school magazines) of 1924 when compared with those of 1894. This method of documentary analysis was to become known later as content analysis and is discussed later, in chapter 6.

But the importance of the Lynds' work lies neither in their methods nor in their results. The importance of their work for sociology was primarily that they were the first sociologists actually to state their methods. They give them in an appendix. Before the Lynds, sociologists had never clearly stated their methods, relying on hints and footnotes. It had never been considered necessary. The pre-eminence of Chicago may have had much to do with this. Most sociologists were Chicago graduates and consequently when communicating with other sociologists they had no need to state their methods, all had a common background. Park's journalistic training may also have encouraged this lack. He wanted to produce works that the general public could read and this meant that the technicalities of methods were excluded. Lynd, as an outsider, was not subject to these influences and so published his methods. As a corollary to this Lynd also was very meticulous in his citation of sources. After reading numerous studies of the Chicago school in which references are given by allusion this is very refreshing. It also was necessary for the development of sociology. When there were only a few sources, of which all were aware, the more haphazard citations typical of the Chicago school were acceptable, but the growing body of sociological literature necessitated the more rigorous approach of the Lynds. Another important contribution of the Lynds' study was to turn the sociological method on to the middle classes. The ethnological approach was one of the sources of the origin of middle-class voyeurism, a strong tradition in sociology. It is appropriate that it was anthropology, the child of ethnology, that turned that voyeurism back on the middle classes.

Warner

The next major study of community life after the Lynds was undertaken by Lloyd Warner and his associates. The major importance of this work, published as *The Social Life of a Modern Community* (1941), lies in its conception of social class and it is therefore dealt with in chapter 6, 'Measurement and analysis'. A brief account of the research is all that is needed here. Warner was a Chicago sociologist who was involved in the study of the Hawthorne electric plant in Chicago (see Roethlisberger and Dickson, 1939). Mayo, one of the key research workers, encouraged

Warner to look at the workers' lives outside the factory. Warner wanted, like the Lynds, to use an anthropological approach. Chicago was too big to study in this way and the district the Hawthorne workers came from was perceived as too 'disorganised' for study as a community. He therefore chose to study a New England town, which he called Yankee Town. His theoretical approach was more explicit than the Lynds' and he developed the idea of functionalism by postulating the concept of structure. He saw a variety of structures, such as the family, age-grading and social class, acting as an integrating force in a community. This structural-functionalism was to become a major theoretical interest in American sociology.

The contribution of community studies

Social ecology narrowed the field of study. Community studies enlarged it once again by insisting upon the interconnectedness of all social phenomena. This broadening of perspective, although a necessary reminder to sociologists, did not lead to any great insights into social life as ecology had done. Community studies were important however because they were the first sociological studies to look at the middle classes. The constant refrain of the Lynds and Warner is their difficulty in standing outside their objects of study, the difficulty of remaining detached. This refrain had never appeared in sociology before because only outsiders had been studied.

LAZARSFELD AND ASSOCIATES

The People's Choice (1944), a study of voting intention in Erie County, USA, is a landmark in the development of survey techniques. Its importance lies in the fact that for the first time in a major survey time was introduced as an element in the analysis. Booth had been forced to take account of time in his surveys, but had never treated it as a major variable. Other researchers had felt able to ignore it, because the development of sampling techniques had reduced the time needed to complete surveys.

Lazarsfeld and his associates chose to make time an important variable in the analysis. This meant that for the first time a social survey could, like an experiment, be used to find causes. The idea of causality is complex but is summarised below on a basis of two known variables; for ease of exposition the complications that arise where a third variable's effect is known are not covered.

If a variable 'A' is to be shown as the cause of 'B' three conditions must be fulfilled:

1. A and B must co-vary, i.e. when A changes so does B. This can be demonstrated by some measure of association such as a correlation.
2. A must occur before B. A may occur before B and still not be a cause—for example the rising of the sun occurs before the peak-hour traffic rush but it is not a cause of it in any meaningful sense. However if A does not occur before B then it obviously cannot be a cause of B. To demonstrate this point requires that time be introduced as an element into any research.
3. It must be shown that A and not any other variable causes B. This is the most difficult of all the three conditions to demonstrate. It can be done by:
   (a) experimental control of all the variables;
   (b) randomisation of all the variables; or
   (c) the use of control groups.

Before *The People's Choice* study only the first of these three conditions had been demonstrated in survey research. Shaw, for example, had shown an association between juvenile delinquency and certain areas of the city, not a causal relationship. Lazarsfeld and his colleagues introduced time as an element in their use of a 'survey panel' which consisted of a group of people who were interviewed serveral times over a time-span. They were able also to fulfil the third condition by the use of control groups. These control groups were groups of people interviewed less often than the panel. By the use of control groups it is possible to measure how much of any change in behaviour is the result of the actual interviewing rather than other causes. (This basic problem of social research, that by measuring one changes what one measures, has already been discussed in chapter 2 and will be met with again in chapter 7, so there is no need to labour it here.)

Before looking in detail at how the research was carried out it is useful to look at its antecedents. The idea of looking at voting behaviour has its origins in the work of Condorcet. It was not fully developed however until Gallup's work in the 1930s. American sociologists and thinkers were worried about the implications of a 'mass society'. This fear of a 'mass society' found form in Ortega y Gassett's writings in Europe in the 1930s. It was to re-emerge as a theme during and after the Second World War in the works of Erich Fromm (1942) and David Riesman *et al.* (1950). In the 1920s in America however it became a concern with propaganda—how men had their opinions moulded by the mass media. Walter Lippman's *Public Opinion* (1922) had drawn attention to the field and in 1930 Gallup applied the well developed techniques of sampling theory to the measurement of public opinion. This public opinion polling became an important feature of American political life. Lundberg (1945) saw it as the saviour of democracy:

> It may be that through properly administered public opinion polls professionalized public officials can give us the efficient government now claimed for authoritarian, centralized administration and yet have that administration at all times subject to the dictates of a more delicate barometer of the people's will than is provided by all the technologically obsolete paraphernalia of traditional democratic processes (p. 507).

The shades of positivism are very apparent in this quotation from Lundberg with its belief that social science can lead to a more rational government. Public opinion polling also became an important part of American sociology. Lazarsfeld was one of the first people to see in this technique the possibility of money for sociological research. He managed to create at Columbia a research institute which carried out work for commercial interests. These research institutes are now fairly common in American university life and have, as Lazarsfeld (1962) argues, an important effect upon sociology, creating a methodological sophistication previously lacking:

> Now, supervising even a small research staff makes one acutely aware of the differences between various elements of a research operation and of the need to integrate them into a final product. Some assistants are best at detailed interviews, others are gifted in the handling of statistical tables, still others are especially good at searching for possible contributions from existing literature. The different roles must be made explicit; each has to know what is expected of him and how his task is related to the work of the others. Thus, staff instruction quickly turns into methodological explication. Maintaining the intellectual standards of an institute is tantamount to codifying empirical social research as an autonomous intellectual world (p. 758).

Certainly *The People's Choice* is far more methodologically sophisticated than previous works. The idea of panel analysis had been developed in the commercial work of the Institute: the first account of panel analysis given in 1938 by Lazarsfeld and Fiske relies heavily on a study undertaken concerning the readership of a women's magazine, *Woman's Home Companion*, to illustrate the technique.

The idea of looking at two sets of responses at different points in time had not originated with Lazarsfeld. As early as 1927 Donald Young had tried to assess the effectiveness of a course on race relations by measuring attitudes at the beginning of the course and at the end of the course. Rice (1928) reports a study he did on voting intentions, in which he looked at the political attitudes of students at Dartmouth on a scale ordering Radicalism, Liberalism, Conservatism, Reactionaryism and related these attitudes to voting intentions in October and at the date of the election in November. Rice was a Columbia graduate and he may have had some influence on Lazarsfeld, who taught at Columbia. Both Young and Rice aggregated their results to look at percentage changes. In so doing they lost the opportunity to go into the detailed influences that led to the changes. Lazarsfeld and his associates looked at the individual. This stress on the individual probably came from opinion polling in which each individual's response counted equally in the final sum—incidentally an assumption that is not justified except in voting studies. It was not only the emphasis on the individual that set off the approach developed by Lazarsfeld. It was the fact that the individual was interviewed and asked what had influenced his choice. In this way the causes of choice could be ascertained rather than a recording of the changes in choice patterns of groups.

The research method used was to draw out a representative sample of voters in Erie County, Ohio, by visiting every fourth house. This produced a 'poll' of 6,000 people. From this 'poll' four samples of 600 people were drawn, each of which was chosen to represent the 'poll' sample and thus the voting population of Erie County. These four samples were called the panel and control groups A, B and C. The panel was interviewed every month for seven months from May to November 1940. Control group A was interviewed in July and control group B in August—at the time of the party conventions. Control group C was interviewed in October just before the election. The interviews were undertaken to see if people changed their voting intentions (77 per cent did not change) and, if they had changed, what their reasons were; to see what exposure they had had to campaign propaganda from the mass media and family and friends, and to discover the personal characteristics of the respondents. This intensive study enabled the researchers to relate, as many had done before them, voting intentions to socio-economic status, occupation, religion, age and residence in rural or urban areas. More important, by cross-classifying variables in a time sequence they could seek the origins of voting intentions. As they say, 'we did not describe opinion; we studied it *in the making*' (Lazarsfeld *et al.*, 1948, p. x).

An example of their technique can be found in chapter 6 of *The People's Choice* which looks at the influences which act to determine when a person will make a final decision to vote in a certain way. They distinguish two major influences: 'interest' and 'cross-pressures'. Those with less interest in the campaign decided later than others who to vote for. Those who were subject to cross-pressures decided later than those who were not. They mean by cross-pressures an inconsistency between factors which influence voting, e.g. people of high social class tend to vote Republican and Catholics tend to vote Democrat; a Catholic of high social class is therefore under a cross-pressure. They are then able to look at people of differing level of interest, with differing cross-pressures, over time to see when they decide to vote. The result is a complex chart (see figure 8) which shows clearly

People who are exposed to cross-pressures delay their final vote decision. This is true separately for people with great interest and for those with less interest. The effect of the cross-pressure is illustrated in each pair of bars.

This chart represents those with great interest.

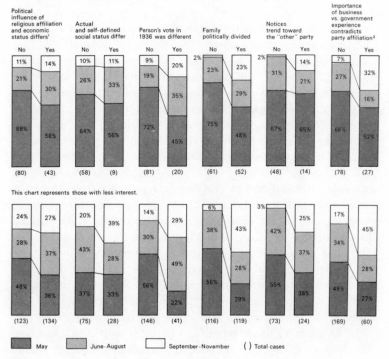

1 Poor Protestants or rich Catholics

2 Republicans who think a candidate needs government experience (which Willkie had not),
or Democrats who think business experience is needed (which Roosevelt had not).

figure 8

that when interest is held constant people who are exposed to cross-pressures delay their decision on who to vote for, i.e. people with cross-pressures who show great interest delay their decision more than those without cross-pressures and great interest, and the same is true for those with little interest.

The different influence of cross-pressures and interest is teased out in this manner so that the chapter concludes with the statement: 'Great interest tends to bring a decision *as such* whereas lack of conflicting pressures brings a decision *for* one or the other party' (*ibid.*, p. 64).

This type of analysis is undertaken for a whole series of variables and enabled the researchers to reach the conclusion that the most important influence on uncommitted voters was their conversations with friends and workmates: personal influence rather than the influence of the mass media. In this manner they were able to use the survey to find the causes of behaviour: 'The repeated interview technique allows us to establish a time sequence and therefore greatly facilitates causal analysis' (*ibid.*, p. 7).

The contribution of the 'People's Choice' study

The methodological sophistication of Lazarsfeld and his associates made the survey an analytic rather than a descriptive method. By their introduction of time as an element in surveys they were able to use the survey to discover the causes of social behaviour rather than just the patterns of behaviour. Their use of control groups, although it only excluded the variables introduced by interviewing, was also an advance in that it also allowed a search for causes.

SUMMARY

The social survey was developed to describe the conditions of the poor. The influence of Bentham had led, in England, to the growth of a tradition of fact collecting, by Royal Commissions and censuses, which facilitated efficient administration. To convince administrators of social problems it therefore became necessary to present them with an accumulation of facts. The social survey was developed for this purpose by Charles Booth. This self-imposed task led Booth, and many others, to the realisation that poverty had to be explained in social rather than individual terms. Booth's pioneering work was developed and extended by British workers throughout the twentieth century. The most important development was Bowley's use of sampling, which led to a faster method of surveying an area. In the United States of America Booth's work was replicated in the Pittsburgh Survey of Paul Kellogg and his associates. This work, and Booth's influenced Robert Park and Ernest Burgess, key figures in the development of the sociology department at Chicago. From these and other sources they developed, with their graduate students, two sociological fields of interest: urban ecology and community studies. Urban ecology— the study of the city as an ecological system—led to many insights, particularly in the field of criminology. Its importance for the development of the social survey was that it was analytic. It sought to relate a particular variable to other variables and in so doing developed techniques of measurement and analysis. Community studies were important because for the first time a sociological method, the social survey, was applied to the study of the middle classes. The impetus for community studies, as well as coming from the ecological approach, came also from anthropology with its functionalist perspective. Booth had tried to describe a social phenomenon, poverty, and had additionally discovered some of its concomitants. The ecologists concentrated on particular social phenomena—crime, suicide, prostitution—and were directly concerned with their concomitants. It was not until Lazarsfeld and his fellow workers became interested in voting behaviour that the social survey was used to find causes. By the use of repeated interviewing of a panel of respondents over a seven-month interval they were able to show the causes of changes in behaviour. With their work the survey became an experimental method.

Participant observation and life histories

Although the term *observer* suggests passivity, a participant observer in the field is at once reporter, interviewer and scientist. On the scene, he gets the story of an event by questioning participants about what is happening and why. He fills out the story by asking people about their relation to the event, their reactions, opinions and evaluation of its significance. As interviewer, he encourages an informant to tell his story or supply an expert account of an organization or group. As scientist, he seeks answers to questions, setting up hypotheses and collecting the data with which to test them. Geer (quoted in Hammond, 1964, p. 331).

The methods of participant observation and the use of life histories have in common a concern with seeing the world from the point of view of the person or group that is being studied. The emphasis is on the subjective and the intuitive. The attempt is made, in both methods, to empathise with those being studied so that one can understand them and their behaviour. In this respect, as well as others, both are more akin to art than science. The distinction between accounts written by participant observers and accounts written by good journalists is indefinite and blurred. Similarly the autobiography and the life history are distinguishable only by the focus of their study: the autobiography is written by a middle-class person about his life, the life history is written by a working-class person about his life. Now that working-class people write autobiographies the distinction between life history and auto-biography is almost impossible to make—the works of Frank Norman (e.g. *Banana Boy*, 1969) are a case in point.

It is not only in the way they are written up that these research methods are not scientific. If it were just a matter of style it would be better for scientists to imitate the style of the sociologists who use these methods rather than vice versa. It is however more than that. Participant observation is inherently non-scientific. It has often been argued that it is non-scientific because it relies on the subjective judgments of the observers. This is not a point I wish to discuss here. All science is ultimately subjective: the most sophisticated measuring instruments require a human eye and brain to interpret them, the judgment of whether a needle crosses a black line is easier to make than whether a person is enjoying himself, but it is a judgment nonetheless. It is not the subjective nature of participant observation that makes it non-scientific but the fact that its methods are not subject to public scrutiny. The essence of a science is that the methods used in it can be presented to other scientists for scrutiny and, if they wish, for replication. The intuitive nature of participant observation precludes this. It is often not possible to know how one acquired items of information, insights and hypotheses in a participant observation study, and it is certainly impossible to present them all for others to examine. Any work which attempted this would be of inordinate length. The life history avoids this problem by confining the research to one person. In this way all, or nearly all, the significant events, as he sees them, can be presented.

The life history is non-scientific in another way. Like the comparative method of looking at history which is discussed in the next chapter, it deals with unique events. In this case unique individuals. One of the requirements of a science is that it deal with regularities. The life history is by definition unique, so regularities cannot be found, though they might be suggested for testing in another way. A collection of life histories, like a collection of community studies, could be used to find regularities but there have been no attempts to do this.

The essentially artistic nature of these methods means that no clear line of progress can be traced in their techniques, as was the case with the experiment and the survey. Works written in 1920 used essentially the same method as works written in 1970. The only progress has been in the realisation of the limitations of the methods for generalisations and their advantages for suggesting propositions to be tested more rigorously in experiments or surveys. Before looking at specific studies that use each method I want to look briefly at the origins of each method and the debate about their merits vis-à-vis the survey or the experiment which reached its peak about 1940.

Participant observation had its origins in the work of Booth. His curiosity about and compassion for the urban poor led him to live in poor areas, the better to understand the people in them. It was not until the 1920s that his example was followed by others in Chicago. Park, one of the major figures in sociology in Chicago, was a journalist, and this may have led him to encourage his students to adopt participant observation as a method. Other influences could have come from anthropology. In 1922, Malinowski published his *Argonauts of the Western Pacific*, in the introduction of which he sets out clearly the method of participant observation. This introduction remains the most succinct summary of the problems and advantages of participant observation, though Malinowski never used the term. He pointed out that there were no historians in a primitive tribe and so the anthropologist has to look at the concrete actions of the people and draw his own inferences from these actions. To achieve this he must look at *all* actions, not just those which appear quaint and unusual. He suggested that a research worker should keep a diary in which to record all observations. By keeping a diary an observer retains his first impressions of a tribe which may be blotted out once he has lived with them for some time. He also stresses that the observer should listen to what people say, and when listening should be looking for evidence of rules of conduct rather than trying to understand individual feelings. By these methods Malinowski suggested that it was possible to grasp the natives' view of the world and understand it.

It must have been obvious to those Chicago students who read Malinowski that they faced very similar problems to Malinowski in trying to understand working-class areas in Chicago. Those areas, like Malinowski's tribes, had no historians and possessed their own values and norms. Whatever the influences on the Chicago sociologists, anthropology or journalism or both, they produced a series of works that remain important in their use of participant observation. Anderson's (1923) study of hobos (he had himself been a hobo), was the first in a series of studies of working-class and criminal life in Chicago. This work was closely followed by Thrasher's study of gangs which established participant observation as a sociological method. The term 'participant observation' was coined by Lindeman (1924), a Chicago sociologist, in his book on sociological methods, *Social Discovery*. He coined the phrase 'participant observer' to describe individuals who belong to a group and report on that group to investigators: 'For experimental purposes the cooperating observers have been called *"participant observers"* ' (p. 191). For Lindeman a participant observer was someone who 'has vital interests involved in the group's activities [and] corrects conclusions of the outside observer from the point of view of one whose interests are at stake' (*ibid.*, p. 192). Such a definition differs from the meaning given to the term today. A participant observer today is usually a sociologist who joins a group to observe it. The type of individual described by Lindeman would now be called 'an informant', but the phrase coined by Lindeman remains.

The life history as a research method emerged with participant observation and ecology as yet another method of the Chicago School. Life histories had formed part of the Chicago tradition from the time of the pioneering work of Thomas and Znaniecki (1927) on Polish peasants and their assimilation into American life. It was the work of Shaw that brought it into prominence as a sociological method however with the publication of *The Jack Roller* (1930), followed by *The Natural History of a Delinquent Career* (1931) and *Brothers in Crime* (1938). The life history formed part of many other sociological studies. It was seen as a 'social microscope' by Burgess (in Gottschalk *et al*, 1945):

The place of the life history in sociology may be better understood by an analysis of the nature of the microscope as an instrument of research in biology. The principle of the microscope is simple, that of enlargement, so that what was previously invisible to the naked eye may be clearly perceived. The great discoveries which the microscope has made possible—the activities of bacteria and other microorganisms—result from observation through lenses that magnify. Persons must, of course, be trained to make accurate and discriminating observation. Auxiliary instruments must be devised like the slide, the smear, and the culture. But the essential need which the microscope met in the biological sciences was to get beneath the surface of the externally observable to what could not be perceived without its use.

In the psychological and social sciences there is also the necessity of penetrating underneath the surface of the readily observable in human behavior. The basic nature of mind and society is communication, both the intercommunication which goes on between man and his fellows and internal communication which is called thinking. Therefore an instrument is needed for psychological and sociological research which provides the investigator access to the inner life of the person and to the web of intercommunications between persons. This is the virtue of the personal document that it is the record of a personal communication, which like the finding of the microscope recorded upon a slide provides an objective record of behavior. In the case of the microscope it is physiological behavior. In the case of the personal document it is mental and social behavior (pp. 25–6).

In spite of claims such as Burgess's, the life history has declined as a sociological method. The reasons for this decline were twofold. First, it was realised that a life history was a unique document and could not be used to seek out regularities in social life. Secondly it was shown that other methods were able to elicit data with as much insight as that given by the life history without all the work involved. In the same year (1930) that Shaw's *Jack Roller* appeared Stouffer produced a doctorate thesis in which he compared attitude scales with life history documents. He persuaded hundreds of students to write autobiographies, asking them to include all items relevant to prohibition and alcohol. He then submitted these life histories to a panel of judges who assessed the attitude of each writer to prohibition. Stouffer had also given the students a short attitude scale relating to prohibition. A comparison of the results of the attitude scale and the life history assessment showed no real difference and it is quicker to score attitude scales than life histories. In spite of Stouffer's work the decline was not rapid, and a conference held in 1939 was still debating the efficacy of the life history and the survey. It was not until the tremendous development of attitude scales in the American Soldier studies (discussed in chapter 6) that the life history method was finally abandoned. It is interesting to note that Shaw (1930), who was the major exponent of the life history, saw it as an early stage in the understanding of delinquent attitudes:

> While quantitative methods are applicable to a wide range of the more formal aspects of delinquent conduct, some more discerning, though perhaps less exact, method is necessary to disclose the underlying processes involved in the formation of delinquent behavior trends. Perhaps with the further refinement of such techniques as the questionnaire and personality rating scales, many aspects of delinquent behavior which we now study by means of personal documents will be subject to more objective analysis (p. 21).

PARTICIPANT OBSERVATION

Anderson, Thrasher and Cressey

Anderson's (1923) study of the hobo area of Chicago was the first of the Chicago participant observation studies and its importance lies in this fact rather than any other contribution it made to sociology. Anderson had been a hobo and in this he differs from most participant observers who are academics who go and live with the people they want to study. He was a hobo who became an academic. His study was financed with a small grant of $300 by a local doctor who had a humanitarian concern for the hobos. The study was important as a trail-blazer. The reaction to it illustrates the voyeurism implicit in most participant observation studies:

> Hobo areas of Chicago were among the least-visited parts of the city, and many readers outside the profession of sociology found the descriptions almost romantically interesting. While ordinary tourists

coming to Chicago usually visited parks and museums . . . it was the University which provided tours for visiting students to such places as Hobohemia, and for a time slumming visits were a fashion among young Chicago intellectuals. Picturesque faces could be seen there in greater variety than in any other part of the city, and the sight of the strange establishments—the employment agencies, the flophouses, the lady barbers, the burlesque shows, the pawnshops—were the next thing in local color to a trip abroad (Faris, 1967, p. 65).

More important for participant observation than Anderson's pioneer work was the work of Thrasher. An account of how he operated is given in Thrasher (1928). His study of gangs has already been mentioned in connection with urban ecology. It was a study that was also important for participant observation. Thrasher spent seven years on his study much of the time actually engaged in participant observation in gangs. This gave him time to gain their confidence and thus look 'below the surface' of their lives. He was able consequently to explain the structure of roles in the gang, and it is this aspect which will be illustrated here because it foreshadows the work of W. F. Whyte discussed later. Thrasher distinguishes the roles of 'leader', the 'brain', the 'funny boy', the 'sissy', the 'show-off' and the 'goat'. A quotation describing the 'goat' captures the flavour of Thrasher's (1927) book, which appears to cram in a great deal of thought into a short space, before going rapidly on to the next item:

Every gang usually has its 'goat'. He is a boy who is considered uncommonly 'dumb'; he may be subnormal, as measured by psychological tests; and he can usually be depended upon to get caught if anybody does. Boys of this type are sometimes known as 'goofy guys', if they combine some special peculiarity with their dumbness. Inexperienced boys are often used as 'cat's-paws' in the exploits of the gang (1963 edn, p. 234).

The work which most clearly illustrates the participant observation method at its best however was that undertaken by Paul Cressey for the Juvenile Protection Agency in Chicago. He was asked to look at 'the taxi-dance halls' in which men hired girls for the duration of a dance. There were no records of this institution so Cressey originally tried to interview the proprietors of the dance-halls. They would not cooperate so he developed the idea of sending in observers to participate in the activities of the taxi-dance hall. From this he obtained an understanding of the taxi-dance hall which showed great sociological insight. Once again, an example must suffice. In a section entitled 'The exploitation motif' Cressey (1932) discusses what he called 'schemes of life'. These are the ways in which individuals in the dance-hall seek to achieve what they consider to be significant in life. He sees these schemes of life as being associated with a 'philosophy of life' which seeks to rationalise the scheme of life adopted by the person concerned:

> The dominant scheme of life for both patrons and taxi-dancers grows out of the combined commercial and romantic interests and the necessary casual intimacies with many patrons. It is represented in the motive of exploitation toward the other sex, prominent in the minds of the most seasoned taxi-dancers and of not a few patrons.
>
> An important aspect of the scheme of life is the attitude which taxi-dancer and patron adopt toward each other. The impersonal attitudes of the market place very soon supersede the romantic impulses which normally might develop. Under the spur of commercialism the taxi-dancer, for instance, very soon comes to view the patrons, young or old, not so much as *ends*, but rather as *means* toward the achievement of her objectives—the recouping of her personal fortunes. Romantic behavior, along with other less desirable forms of stimulation, becomes merely another acceptable method for the commercial exploitation of the men.
>
> The patron's point of view is the complement of the taxi-dancer's. He is interested in securing an attractive young woman with whom he may dance and converse without the formality of an introduction and without many of the responsibilities entailed at other social gatherings. Frequently he desires a young woman who gives promises of other contacts later in the night. Thus, from the special interests of the patrons and the commercial aims of the taxi-dancer a competitive struggle develops between man and woman for an advantage over each other. In many instances the struggle is a conscious one in

which any means, fair or foul, are used in exploiting the other. 'All these girls are after is the money they think they can get out of a fellow. They'll "gyp" a guy if they can. But they don't get far wid me. I'm on to them. . . . But it's not that I care about. I can take care of myself. I'm not just trying to keep them from putting something over on me; I'm trying to put it over on them. I know what I'm after and I'm out to get it. That's me all over' (Conversation of a patron with an investigator.) . . .

Neither taxi-dancer nor most patrons perceive that the most basic explanation for these unfortunate associations, these unpleasant experiences, is to be found not so much in the original character of the individuals themselves as in the very social structure of the present-day taxi-dance hall.

Unable to perceive these basic yet unseen social forces which shape her life, the taxi-dancer becomes something of a drifter, gaining what satisfactions she can from the transient thrills of the day and from the skilful practising of her devices for exploitation (pp. 39–41).

Cressey's work has been extensively quoted to show how little participant observation has changed since 1930. It is interesting to compare the above extract with the quotation from Becker's work published in 1951 which is given on pages 99 and 100. Both show a similar incisive grasp of the subtleties of social interaction.

Whyte
One of the most interesting and influential pieces of participant observation research ever done was done by William Whyte in Boston. He studied a slum neighbourhood occupied by Italian immigrants. The results of his study remain important in sociology. He demonstrated, in detail, the patterns of interaction in a street corner gang. This demonstration of structure in gangs was important in two ways. First he demonstrated that the slum areas were not, as the urban ecologists had presumed, areas devoid of any social organisation. They had their own social structure, norms and patterns of behaviour. These structures, norms and patterns restricted them just as ordinary society was restricted by its structures, norms and behaviour patterns. Secondly, and more

important, his detailed description of interaction patterns provided a source which later theorists were to tap time and time again. His description of the behavioural concomitants of leadership has been particularly important. He demonstrated that 'Doc', the leader of the street corner gang, always gave out more money and favours than he received. He also showed that the scores of individual gang members at ten-pin bowling were related to their position in the gang: the leaders consistently doing better than those lower down. These findings were influential in the development both of Homans's (1951) theories of group behaviour and in the development of Blau's (1964) exchange theory of social life.

Although the results of the study were influential, the impact of the book on participant observation research was its most interesting aspect. Whyte, in an appendix, gives what appears to be a very honest account of his reasons for conducting the research and the problems and difficulties he encountered. He went into the research for several reasons. He had originally wanted to be a writer but had found that his own background did not supply him with sufficient experience. He came from an upper-middle-class background which limited the scope of his plays, novels and short stories. He decided therefore that he would like to live outside his 'own people', as it were, to gain experience. He also wanted to reform the slums of the big cities. He had visited slum districts while at university and was appalled at the conditions in them. Like Booth he had tried political action to achieve reforms; in his case he tried to change the university in which he was an undergraduate. Like Booth he failed and consequently sought other means than politics to achieve reform. (Later, while in the slum district he called 'Cornerville', he did take part in political action, but his study grew, in part, out of his realisation of the difficulties of achieving reforms he had encountered in his undergraduate days.)

He gained a fellowship from Harvard which financed his study. He originally intended and planned a massive economic study of housing conditions, but his supervisor pointed out that he had not got the experience to supervise such an ambitious project. He then persuaded a friend, John Howard, to work with him as a member of his field staff. However by the time Howard joined him he had already begun to live in Cornerville and his orientation had become more and more sociological and anthropological, less and less economic. He specifically mentions the reading of Malinowski's work as an influence on his thoughts. Another important influence predisposing him to anthropology was Conrad Arensberg. Arensberg had worked with Lloyd Warner in his Yankee City studies and also completed a study of a small community in Ireland both of which were anthropological in tone. Arensberg, like Whyte, was a junior Harvard fellow and they discussed Whyte's research together. As well as this account of his reasons for undertaking the research, Whyte (1943) gives an account of the method of participant observation that remains as the first full account of the method and as one of the best accounts of the method:

> In describing my Cornerville study, I have often said I was three months in the field before I knew where my research was going (p. 321).
> ... The ideas that we have in research are only in part a logical product growing out of a careful weighing of evidence. We do not generally think problems through in a straight line. Often we have the experience of being immersed in a mass of confusing data. We study the data carefully, bringing all our powers of logical analysis to bear upon them. We come up with an idea or two. But still the data do not fall into any coherent pattern. Then we go on living with the data—and with the people—until perhaps some chance occurrence casts a totally different light upon the data, and we begin to see a pattern that we have not seen before. This pattern is not purely an artistic creation. Once we think we see it, we must re-examine our notes and perhaps set out to gather new data in order to determine whether the pattern adequately represents the life we are observing or is simply a product of our imagination. Logic, then, plays an important part. But I am convinced that the actual evolution of research ideas does not take place in accord with the formal statements we read on research methods. The ideas grow up in part out of our immersion in the data and out of the whole process of living. Since

97

so much of this process of analysis proceeds on the unconscious level, I am sure that we can never present a full account of it (p. 279).

He insists that only close contact with the people one studies can give the insight necessary for good participant observation:

> Life in Cornerville did not proceed on the basis of formal appointments. To meet people, to get to know them, to fit into their activities, required spending time with them—a lot of time day after day. . . . You might find the time passing entirely uneventfully. You might just be standing around with people whose only occupation was talking or walking about to try to keep themselves from being bored (p. 293).
> . . . Sometimes I wondered whether just hanging on the street corner was an active enough process to be dignified by the term 'research' (p. 303).
> . . . [The research] took a long time because the parts of the study that interest me most depended upon an intimate familiarity with people and situations. . . . This familiarity gave rise to the basic ideas in this book. I did not develop these ideas by any strict logical process. They dawned on me out of what I was seeing, hearing, doing—and feeling. They grew out of an effort to organise a confusing welter of experience (pp. 356–7).

Whyte is also astute enough to realise the advantages of the method over interviews and questionnaires: his main informant, Doc, had told him: ' "If people accept you, you can just hang around, and you'll learn the answers in the long run without even having to ask the questions" ', and he was sensible enough to take this advice: 'As I sat and listened, I learned the answers to questions that I would not even have had the sense to ask if I had been getting my information solely on an interviewing basis' (p. 303). This 'overhearing' technique is one of the great advantages of participant observation. The Webbs (1932) in their discussion of research methods mention it as an important technique and Becker (1958) regards it as very important because there is likely to be less distortion in an overheard statement than in a direct statement to an interviewer or participant observer.

Whyte provided in his appendix an explanation of the method

of participant observation and a justification for it in exploratory research. It is for this, as well as the substantive results of his research, that he should be remembered.

Howard Becker

As well as substantive research on medical students (1961), dance musicians (1951), marihuana users (1953) and public schoolteachers (1952) and theoretical writings based on these studies, for example a discussion of the concept of career (1956, with A.L. Strauss), Becker has produced several discussions of participant observation as a research method (1945, 1957, 1958 and 1960). He is a great supporter of participant observation as a method, arguing that it is possible to construct and test hypotheses using the method equally as rigorous as the hypotheses constructed and used by those who use statistical methods. In fact, in a most bitter attack on behaviourists (1945), he argues that participant observation may be better than observation of actions because it reveals the motives behind men's actions and thus fulfils Weber's demand for explanation on the level of meaning as well as enabling better predictions to be made. He is aware also however of the shortcomings of the method:

> The data of participant observation . . . frequently consist of many different kinds of observations which cannot be simply categorized and counted without losing some of their value as evidence—for . . . many points need to be taken into account in putting each datum to use. Yet it is clearly out of the question to publish all the evidence. Nor is it any solution . . . to publish a short version and to make available the entire set of materials on microfilm or in some other inexpensive way; this ignores the problem of how to present *proof* (1958, pp. 659–60).

In his own use of the method he demonstrates an intuitive grasp of the processes of social interaction and an ability to express these complex processes simply and tellingly. An example of his work illustrates these points:

> The musician is conceived of by the professional group as an artist who possesses a mysterious artistic gift setting him apart from all

other people. Possessing this gift, he should be free from control by, outsiders who lack it . . .

This attitude is generalized into a feeling that musicians are completely different from and better than other kinds of people and accordingly ought not to be subject to the control of outsiders in any branch of life, particularly in their artistic activity . . .

From the idea that no one can tell a musician how to play it follows logically that no one can tell a musician how to do anything. Accordingly, behavior which flouts conventional social norms is greatly admired. . . . This is more than idiosyncrasy; it is a primary occupational value . . .

As they do not wish to be forced to live in terms of social conventions, so musicians do not attempt to force these conventions on others. For example, a musician declared that ethnic discrimination is wrong, since every person is entitled to act and believe as he wants to (1951, p. 137).

One can see here a similar attempt to that of Cressey to find the philosophy of life which guides the scheme of life adopted by the members of an occupational group. It is in this search for the meanings men give to the social world around them that the method of participant observation contributes most to sociology both in the development of theory and in substantive findings.

Mass observation
One of the most interesting uses of participant observation was known under the title of 'mass observation'. This was a self-conscious attempt to apply the methods of anthropology to a modern industrial society: Britain. Its main inspiration came from Tom Harrisson. Harrisson was a dedicated and enthusiastic ornothologist who before he left school had published a book on the birds in the Harrow district and accompanied an Oxford University expedition to the Arctic. On an expedition to St Kilda, which he organised, the following year he became interested in people as well as birds as an object of study. An expedition to Borneo enabled him to live among primitive tribes and study them. This was followed by further anthropological expeditions to various parts of the world during which he realised that much of

British life had never been studied and was as unknown as that of these primitive tribes. He decided therefore to apply anthropological methods to British society. He was supported in this task by a former *Mirror* reporter Charles Madge who had become concerned about the gap between the ordinary people and the news media. As in Chicago, the conjunction of anthropology and journalism produced a research design which employed participant observation.

The method adopted by Harrisson and Madge was to have a network of participant observers throughout Britain keeping diaries and observations which they sent up to a central office where they were analysed. These observers were all volunteers recruited in answer to a request for help made in letters to the national newspapers. Originally, on 12 February 1937 there were only thirty observers. By 12 May there were hundreds, by the end of 1938 there were thousands. In addition to these volunteers there were also full-time observers looking at two areas in detail: a typical northern industrial town and a metropolitan London borough.

The first study asked the observers merely to note down everything that happened to them on 12 February 1937. On 12 May the same procedure was followed with the difference that this was a coronation day (published as *May 12th*, 1937). The first study by the full-time observers concentrated on the major leisure activities of the working class: smoking, pub-going and football pools (*First Year's Work*, 1938). In the same year an account of the reactions of ordinary people to international crisis was undertaken and remains a useful historical account of that period (*Britain*, 1938). With the outbreak of war the focus turned on what was later to be called the 'home front' (*War Begins at Home*, 1940). All these, and other later studies, used a variety of techniques. As well as participant observation of particular events and the reaction of people to them, there were accounts by observers of a full day, surveys of a more formal kind, with interviews and questionnaires, and content analysis of documents.

All this effort was extremely impressive but the result was much less so. The results produced by Mass Observation remain as a useful source material for historians, they are of little interest to sociology, except as an example of a lost opportunity. The participant observation method when it is used in anthropology, or in sociology, relies upon an interaction in the observer's mind between the data he observes and collects and the theoretical ideas he has at his disposal. If it works, this interaction can be very fruitful. Observation suggests theoretical ideas which can be tested by further observation which may in turn suggest new theoretical explanations. The fault with Mass Observation was that it confused the observation of events by participants with participant observation. The observers were participant observers in Lindeman's sense, i.e. they were informants. Their information was useful but it needed to be placed in a theoretical context. This Harrisson and Madge failed to do and this is why their work remains a sociological oddity rather than the important work it might have been.

A LIFE HISTORY

Shaw has already been mentioned in connection with his ecological studies. He also presented several life histories of which *The Jack Roller* (1930), a study of a boy named Stanley, was the first. He was as rigorous in his use of life history material as he had been in his statistical ecological studies and his use of life histories remain models for the method. *The Jack Roller* presents not only the boy's own story but also other data which put it into context. Thus, before the story is presented in the boy's words, the reader is given a full list of his arrests and commitments and a full list of his school and work record in so far as these could be independently checked. In addition the areas Stanley lived in are described with particular reference to their juvenile delinquency rates and his family is described in detail. Appendices give a summary of clinical findings and the original life history the boy produced before extending it at the request of Shaw.

Shaw's method of eliciting life histories was arduous. He first obtained a complete list of Stanley's arrests and committals. These were presented to Stanley who was asked to tell Shaw his life story; this was recorded verbatim, by a stenographer. He was then asked to expand this story giving more detailed descriptions. This process took six years. Throughout the boy's statements were measured against objective evidence where it was available. Shaw's interest in the life history was both reformist and sociological. Using the life history written by Stanley, Shaw deduced his personality needs and found him a job, as a salesman, that fitted those needs thus helping him to reform.

The sociological function of life histories as stated by Shaw (1930) was that:

> They not only serve as a means of making preliminary explorations and orientations in relation to specific problems in the field of criminological research but afford a basis for the formulation of hypotheses with reference to the causal factors involved in the development of delinquent behavior patterns. The validity of these hypotheses may in turn be tested by the comparative study of other detailed case histories and by formal methods of statistical analysis (p. 19).

Shaw saw the life history as being the source for hypotheses in three areas. The first was the personality and attitudes of delinquents. In this respect he was careful to point out that the biased picture presented by Stanley was part of the interest. The second area that was illuminated was the social world of the delinquent: the norms, values, home-life, neighbourhood of a typical delinquent; the third was the sequence of events in the life of the delinquent. This account of the details of the process of social life is an important area for suggesting hypotheses.

Stanley's life history can be briefly summarised. He came from a broken home. His mother had died and his father had remarried. Stanley hated his stepmother and continually ran away from home and school. Because of this he was sent to a series of institutions. In them he met other, older, delinquents and learnt a way of life from them. Between spells in institutions he left home and went begging in the streets. He was caught and sent back to a reformatory each time. Eventually he was introduced to 'jack-rolling' by a friend. This term, which has now been replaced by 'mugging', was slang for stealing from drunks. He was arrested and sent to reformatory for a year but went back to jack-rolling on release. Upon being caught again he was sent to prison where Shaw first met him. His delinquent career was compressed into nine years: he first ran away from home at six and a half, went to a reformatory for a year at fifteen and was released from prison at seventeen and a half. This brief account cannot capture the full flavour of Stanley's own account which has numerous footnotes attached by Shaw putting the account into the context of a theory of criminology. The quotation from the book given below illustrates the technique and gives an idea of Stanley's style:

> The prisoner in charge of the mangle that I worked on was Billy,* a hardened criminal from Chicago. He was eight years my senior, and was in on a five to life sentence as a burglar and 'stick-up' man. Billy took a great liking to me, mostly out of pity, and gave me instructions on how to get on in Pontiac [prison], and how to get by with the police outside. He indelibly impressed two things on my mind.† First, never trust anybody with your affairs in crime. . . . Second, Billy chided me for petty stealing.
> [Shaw's footnotes]
>
> * Billy was a notorious criminal character in Chicago. He was killed in an encounter with the police during the latter part of 1929.
> † Stanley's contact with Billy illustrates the manner in which the code of the adult criminal world is transmitted to the young delinquent. Through such contacts the youthful offender not only becomes identified with the criminal world, but his wishes and ambitions become organised in terms of the values of the adult criminal group (pp. 105–6).

SUMMARY

Neither participant observation nor the life history method have shown any major improvement in technique since their first use. This lack of progress is due in part to their non-scientific nature. Participant observation is essentially intuitive and artistic. The mass of impressions received and categorised by a participant observer are not open to public scrutiny and without such scrutiny it remains non-scientific. The life history is an account of a unique individual. As such it is impossible to generalise from it to discover regularities in social life. The non-scientific nature of these methods does not mean that they are sociologically useless. They are useful firstly as a source of hypotheses to be tested more rigorously in other ways. Secondly they are useful because they put flesh on the analytic bones of sociology.

The comparative method 5

Social research is, for the moment, not practical and empirical enough; the only thing it regards as empirical is that which is subject to its own techniques. It neglects history and society itself. In other words, its conception of empiricism and science is altogether too narrow.

Mauss (1962, p. 150)

The comparative method was, until the end of the nineteenth century, if not the only method in sociology, certainly the dominant method. It involves abstracting items from different historical societies in an attempt to find laws of history. Society in the eighteenth and nineteenth centuries was changing from a rural communal society to an urban industrial society. Men wished to understand the changing social world around them and they sought this understanding through history. The historical studies they undertook were, however, unlike previous historical studies. Previous studies had been in the humanist tradition, in which history was seen as a way of understanding contemporary problems: study of the way men acted in the past and study of the consequences of their actions would give guidelines for action in the present. In the new way of looking at history, the comparative method, history was still to be a guide for understanding contemporary problems, not now because men were encountering problems similar to those of the past but because history was the source from which laws about the development of societies could be developed. Historical materials were to be the source from which, by the use of scientific methods, scientific laws of history were to be derived.

The origins of the idea of applying the methods of science to human behaviour have already been discussed in chapter 1. A brief restatement may put the comparative method in the context of the origins of sociology. The world was rapidly changing politically and socially. In seeking to understand these changes some men found humanist and theological explanations inadequate. They turned therefore to scientific thought for the means with which to understand society. Scientific methods were emulated not only because science had been successful in creating understanding of the natural world but also because science had been successful in controlling the natural world. These men wanted not only to understand but also to control the social world just as science gave understanding and control of the material world. As Comte, the initiator of both sociology and the comparative method, said, 'voir pour prevoir, prevoir pour prevenir' ('to see in order to foresee, to foresee in order to anticipate'; quoted in Friedrichs, 1970, p. 177).

This remained the aim of all the users of the comparative method after Comte. Three of these are discussed in this chapter: Marx, Spencer and Sorokin. By the end of the nineteenth century the method, in its original form, had been largely abandoned. Each theorist, although he looked at a similar history, produced different laws of history. It became apparent that it was not as easy as Comte had imagined to apply science to history. The reason for this was indicated in the work of Max Weber, who sought to provide a solution to a problem that had not even been perceived by earlier, and some later, users of the comparative method: the problem of the uniqueness of historical events. His criticisms and proposed solution are also discussed in this chapter. In spite of its apparent failure, and in spite of the criticisms of Weber, the method has not been entirely abandoned in sociology. Two variants of it are still practised and will be discussed later. The first variant is that exemplified in the works of Ogburn and Kahn. Each tried to foresee the future in order to control it by extrapolating trends from the past. Their work, and their conclusions, were however much more circumspect than those of the grand theorists such as Comte, Marx, Spencer or Sorokin. They also tended to be more quantitative. The greater caution of their work can be seen in the following quotation from Kahn and Wiener, *The Year 2000* (1967). The quotation with its expectation that knowledge and intelligence may help men to control their future also demonstrates the position of the work in the tradition of the comparative method:

> Just as the economist hopes to avoid not all the phenomena of business cycles, but only their extreme troughs and depressions, so perhaps we can hope with adequate knowledge and intelligence to control the extreme dips and rises of the cultural cycle [in history]. If man may never be completely in control of his fate, perhaps at least he may rise to partial control (p. 412).

The second variant is in the field of cultural anthropology. This consists of examining different contemporary societies rather than different historical societies in a search for universal laws of human behaviour. This task was greatly facilitated by the creation of 'Human relations area files'. These are in essence, libraries of ethnographic material indexed according to anthropological criteria. It is thus possible, for example, to draw out all information in the category 'family' and compare family systems in many different societies. (The task is made even easier today by the use of computer retrieval systems.) This variant shares many of the same problems and difficulties as the original comparative method.

COMTE

Comte was a student at the Ecole Polytechnique in Paris at the time of Waterloo. This was a high status college for students of the applied sciences and here he was trained as a natural scientist. (It was here also that Le Play studied and graduated as a mining engineer.) This grounding in applied science gave Comte the background from which he developed his ideas of applying science to human society. His own application of what he conceived to be the scientific method to history produced a law of progress: the 'Law of the three stages of intellectual development'. Progress could be seen to have occurred in three stages. The first, or 'theological' stage of intellectual development occurred when men believed in fictitious beings who controlled their lives. This was succeeded by the 'metaphysical' stage when men controlled their lives by abstract ideas such as freedom and liberty. Comte conceived the age he lived in as in the metaphysical stage. The future, third stage, was to be the 'positive' stage when scientific principles would control men's lives. Each of these three intellectual stages, Comte conceived of as being related to material and moral stages in man's history as shown below.

Comte's stages of historical development

Intellectual progress	*Moral progress*	*Material progress*
Theological	Family	Conquest
Metaphysical	State	Defence
Positive	Human race	Industry

Man's moral progress could be charted by an ever wider allegiance to broader social groups. His material progress could be charted by his characteristic activity at each stage: conquering others for possessions, defending possessions and co-operating with others to create possessions. Marx's conception of the workers of the world uniting, with the growth of industry, and the subsequent withering away of the state expresses the same transition from the metaphysical to the positive that Comte expresses. Even Marx's idea of a bourgeois ideology that was to be superseded by scientific laws of history owes not a little to Comte. This is hardly surprising, Marx was a great borrower of other people's ideas, an eclectic who synthesised those disparate ideas in a new theory of history.

KARL MARX

Marx, like Comte and also Spencer, never held an academic position. He was educated at the University of Berlin where he was strongly influenced by Hegel's philosophical ideas. He later went to Paris and was influenced by many French thinkers, among them Comte and Saint-Simon. He fused these two traditions of thought in a brilliant philosophical synthesis that was also an appeal for action. It is almost impossible to summarise Marx's writings. His words have been chewed over so often by politicians, philosophers and sociologists that like the Bible and Shakespeare's works every sentence has acquired connotations and commentaries. The situation is not helped by the fact that, again like the Bible and Shakespeare's works, the works of Marx are an untidy, fragmented, incomplete exposition of views on history, society and political action. In spite of the difficulties a short summary of Marx's work as it relates to the comparative method is given here. He saw the law of history not in man's intellectual development, as Comte had done, but in his material development: 'It is men, who, in developing their material production and their material intercourse, change, along with this their real existence, their thinking and the products of their thinking. Life is not determined by consciousness, but consciousness by life' (quoted—Bottomore and Rubel, 1963, p. 90). Man's history was a history of class struggles and classes were defined by their relationship to the means of production. Men had once owned all their goods in common—a primitive communism. Then had arisen classical societies with their classes of slaves, artisans and nobles which were in turn replaced by feudal societies of warriors, serfs and freemen. As I have done, Marx skates quickly over this section of man's history to arrive at capitalist society. In capitalist society there are two classes only: the capitalists and the workers, often called the bourgeoisie and the proletariat. (It should be noted that one of the difficulties in discussing Marx is the fact that although he insists there are only two classes in a capitalist society, and this is a key point in his argument, in some of his writings he talks of rentiers and peasants as classes of a sort.) The capitalists own the means of production. The workers own only their labour which they sell to the capitalists. When the proletariat revolt and seize power, which Marx saw as inevitable, there will be an end to what Marx liked to call pre-history. The new communist society having only one class would not have class struggles. Marx saw revolution as inevitable because he postulated a scientific law of history: the law of dialectical materialism. This sees all history as a process of struggle between two opposing forces at each stage of history: thesis and antithesis. Each struggle of forces creates a new synthesis which contains within it the seeds for a new thesis and antithesis of a higher order. This struggle between thesis and antithesis is the 'dialectic' part of the law. The 'materialism' comes from Marx's conception of these forces as being social classes which are created by their relationship to the material world, their relationship to the tools of production.

Marx's use of the comparative method remains important not only because of all users of the method he had the most influence on the actual course of history, but also because in developing his ideas of history he developed concepts, such as alienation and the dialectic, which remain very important in sociological thought today. Dialectic may be said to be a key concept in understanding all sociological methods and it will be discussed again in the concluding chapter. The actual predictions Marx made using his law were as successful as those of Comte, which means that they were *not* very successful. The only successful proletarian revolution took place in Russia in 1917, an economically backward country, far from being the developed capitalist economy in which Marx conceived the revolution would take place. A discussion of what constitutes a communist revolution could fill a book but it is apparent that although later 'Marxists' may see communist revolutions in China, Jugoslavia and Cuba they would not be recognised as such by Marx.

SPENCER

Spencer, like Comte, had a training in engineering. Unlike Comte his training was much more practical than theoretical. He was a railway company engineer, a not unusual occupation for a middle-class youth in Derby. Like Comte and Marx he never held any academic posts but unlike them he was accepted and supported by the academic world. The reasons for this acceptance lay in the particular law of history he adduced from his studies. He saw history as an evolutionary process and society as an organism constantly evolving. This evolution was achieved by 'the survival of the fittest' a phrase he used ten years before the publication of Darwin's work. It was a consequence of this theory that governments should not interfere in social life for in so doing they would be interfering in the progress produced by evolution. The poor and the infirm would be weeded out by a process of natural selection if governments did not interfere. This conception of the task of government, namely to leave well alone, fitted in well with the prevailing laissez-faire economic theory of the time, which suggested that free competition in a free market produced the best results for all. This approach to economic life suited successful Victorian businessmen and they were quick to accept also Spencer's similar theories about society in general, especially in the United States. Spencer was so popular in the United States in fact that some states even passed laws for the sterilisation of mental defectives and used his arguments in support of their action.

This rather gloomy picture of Spencer's contribution is not the whole story. He introduced into sociological thought the idea that society could be understood as a collection of institutions, e.g. government, economic life. These institutions were conceived to be interdependent parts of a societal organism. Each institution showed in its evolution increasing size, increasing subdivisions and increasing specialisation. In this respect his ideas were the forerunners of the theoretical approach of functionalism in sociology: Durkheim's conceptions of the division of labour and the transition from 'mechanical' to 'organic' society may well have been derived from Spencer's conceptions of increasing differentiation in institutions and increasing interdependence of the differentiated parts.

SOROKIN

Sorokin differs sharply from the three writers discussed above. First, he wrote his work, *Social and Cultural Dynamics* (1937–41), which used the comparative method, in the twentieth century not the nineteenth. (Earlier works included *The Sociology of Revolution*, 1925.) Secondly he was an academic, and thirdly, although of Russian origin, his work was undertaken in America not Europe. Perhaps the most important difference between Sorokin and Comte, Marx or Spencer was his pessimism. The previous three writers all conceived of society as progressing. Sorokin, like other twentieth-century writers who used the comparative method, such as Spengler and Toynbee, was much more pessimistic. Although he viewed history as cyclical he was convinced that he was writing in an age of decline. Why this pessimism should pervade the writings of the twentieth-century users of the comparative method is difficult to understand. It is usually attributed to the war of 1914–18 but Toynbee, who wrote after the war, is more optimistic than Spengler, who wrote before it. The realisation that men act from irrational rather than rational motives, which was accepted after Freud's work became known, may have had some impact on an optimistic view of human history. Certainly Pareto, who was one of the few sociologists to base a sociology on the irrationality of man, saw history as a constant circulation of elites with no progress at all.

Sorokin's conception of history was, like Comte's, concerned with men's intellectual lives. For Sorokin the division was also into three modes of thinking: the 'ideational', the 'idealistic' and the 'sensate'. Each is related to all aspects of society: the arts, religion, ethics, social organisations and philosophical systems. The ideational is the stage of birth, the idealistic that of maturity and the sensate that of old age and decline. We are at present, according to Sorokin, in a sensate stage. The stages can be understood better by looking at some examples of their concomitants. Art, for example, in an ideational culture would be religious, traditional and symbolic; in an idealistic culture it would be noble, patriotic and educational; and in a sensate culture it would be impressionistic, commercial and professional. The systems of truth held in the three stages also differ. Ideational truth is intuitive, revealed and mystical, whereas sensate truth is empirical, practical and scientific. The three stages are very similar to Comte's, but whereas Comte saw each stage as a law of historical progression, Sorokin saw each as part of a perpetually recurring cycle. (In fact it is never clear in Sorokin's work whether he means a cycle of cultures or an oscillation about the idealistic culture.)

OGBURN

Ogburn initiated a new direction for the comparative method. Before Ogburn's classic work *Recent Social Trends* (1934) all users of the comparative method had worked without funds and in a philosophical speculative manner. Ogburn received a huge grant from the government of President Hoover and the Rockefeller Foundation to direct an exploration of the extent and direction of changes in American society. This financing of what was later to be called 'futurology' arose because the government was committed to economic growth, after the crash of the stockmarket in 1929, and wished to plan for that growth. The basic theoretical position of Ogburn (1951) was that of an evolutionist: 'I claim that the problem of social evolution is solved and that I have played a considerable part in solving it . . . The problem of social evolution is solved by four factors: invention, exponential accumulation, diffusion and adjustment' (p. 151).

Ogburn considered he had solved the problem by his insistence on statistical method. This insistence came from his training at Columbia under Giddings, who was both a social evolutionist and a strong advocate of measurement in sociology. Ogburn was a successful pupil. By his use of statistics Ogburn considered that he had avoided the biases of previous users of the comparative method. He considered that he had achieved what would be called a value neutral position today: 'the Committee's collaborators . . . have striven faithfully to discover what is, and to report their findings uncolored by their personal likes and dislikes' (Ogburn and Odum, 1934, p. xciv). The idea of the study 'was to rule out all opinion unsupported and to accept nothing but reliable conclusions. The idea was that as a multiplication table should be reliable both for the Tory and the Communist, so the conclusion of social trends should be valid alike for the radical and the conservative' (Ogburn, 1951, p. 151).

The report produced under the direction of Ogburn is 1,568 pages long and has with it thirteen volumes of special studies and supporting data! It consists of a collection of monographs on trends in everything from population to the activities of women outside the home. Its predictions from trends are by no means as dated as one might expect. The authors discuss the desalination of sea water, floating island cities to meet growing populations, the problems of a consumer society and the effects of television. Ogburn's own specialist contribution, as distinct from his contribution as a director of the study, is concerned with the effect of inventions. Here, and in other works, he suggests that there are three elements in the process of invention. These are the invention itself, a perceived need and a cultural base. By a cultural base he means the accumulation of knowledge in an area. He argues that the cultural base is more important than the genius of an individual or any perceived need and cites in support of this the almost simultaneous discovery by different people of similar inventions, e.g. the telephone, the sewing machine, the aeroplane and the typewriter. From this argument it would follow that the wider the cultural base the more likelihood of invention and Ogburn showed that this was the case. Inventions, in any field, grow in numbers exponentially: where there were ten last year there will be twenty next year, forty in the next six months after that, eighty in the next three months and so on. Ogburn suggested that this rapid growth in technology was too fast for society and society's culture to adapt to easily. This difference between technological and cultural progress he called 'culture-lag' and he considered this to be an important aspect of modern society:

> The thesis is . . . that the source of most modern social changes today is the material-culture. The material-culture changes force changes in other parts of culture such as social organisation and customs, but these latter parts of culture do not change as quickly. They lag behind the material-culture changes, hence we are living in a period of maladjustment (1951, p. 150).

KAHN

Kahn's work in many respects is similar to that of Ogburn, and his 'future studies' are financed by government and big business for purposes of forward planning. Their theoretical bases are however different. Ogburn was a follower of the theory of social evolution. Kahn relies much more on Sorokin's work. More important than this difference however is a difference in their attribution of causes. Ogburn saw change as being largely caused by technology. Kahn takes a multicausal approach, seeing no one factor as being the prime cause of change. His basic unit is what he calls a 'multifold trend' which contains thirteen elements:

There is a basic, long-term multifold trend toward:
1. Increasingly Sensate (empirical, this-worldly, secular, humanistic, pragmatic, utilitarian, contractual, epicurean or hedonistic, and the like) cultures
2. Bourgeois, bureaucratic, 'meritocratic', democratic (and nationalistic?) elites
3. Accumulation of scientific and technological knowledge
4. Institutionalization of change, especially research, development, innovation, and diffusion
5. Worldwide industrialization and modernization
6. Increasing affluence and (recently) leisure
7. Population growth
8. Urbanization and (soon) the growth of megalopolises
9. Decreasing importance of primary and (recently) secondary occupations
10. Literacy and education
11. Increasing capability for mass destruction
12. Increasing tempo of change
13. Increasing universality of the multifold trend (Kahn and Wiener, 1967, p. 7).

This emphasis on multicausality is much more characteristic of modern users of the comparative method. The emphasis is in part due to a realisation of the inadequacy of causal explanations relying on one variable. It is in part also due to the ability, given by electronic computers, to handle with comparative ease multiple variables. I suspect, in fact, that the second explanation of the use of multivariate analyses today is of more importance than the first.

The actual results of Kahn and Wiener's analysis are very interesting but of less importance here than their methods. These include the extension of present trends which is basically the technique pioneered by Ogburn. They include also 'canonical variations'; by this they mean variations from the expected trend if one element in the trend does not proceed as expected. These variations are expressed as 'scenarios', or short plots of what might happen if a variation does take place. These are quite fascinating. A typical scenario looks at the consequences of a world in disarray. A quotation may illustrate the technique:

> By 1985 the number of nuclear armed states in the world has increased. . . . Following a few years of economic recession, and because Canadian business is increasingly falling into United States hands, a radically anti-American, leftist government achieves power in Canada in early 1986. . . . extensive discrimination leads to steadily worsening relations. . . . In 1988 the United States is asked to remove all bases, radars, and so on, from Canadian soil—and we comply (*ibid.*, p. 291).

PROBLEMS OF THE COMPARATIVE METHOD

There are basically three problems involved in the use of the comparative method:

1. the selection of the units of analysis;
2. the importance of each unit at different historical periods;
3. the uniqueness of history.

The first two are common to all sociological explanations. Every sociological explanation has to simplify reality by dividing it into discrete units. Thus sociologists talk of 'role', 'status', 'power' and 'class', for example. In the comparative method the units are 'ideational cultures' or 'metaphysical eras'. Every sociological explanation has to deal also with the different importance different units may have in different societies. Thus 'power' may be an important explanatory concept in one society, less important in another. Similarly 'social class' may be important in the explanation of one historical period, less important in the next. It is the last problem, the uniqueness of historical events, that is specific to the comparative method and to comparative anthropology. The scientific method is essentially a generalising process. A scientist formulates a hypothesis about one situation and tests it in that situation. He then goes on to test the hypothesis again and again in identical situations. To achieve this he has to find identical situations. This is not as easy in history as it is in the natural world. Each historical event is unique. Historical knowledge is ideographic, scientific knowledge is nomothetic. Sociology, as I pointed out when discussing survey methods, if it is to be a science must find recurring situations. This it can most easily do by concentrating on the present rather than on history.

One sociologist, Max Weber, although he realised the uniqueness of historical events, still wished to study them sociologically. He attempted to do this by ignoring the unique aspects of an historical event so that he could generalise about them. In the same way sociologists studying relationships in small groups ignore the unique aspect of each relationship in order to study, abstractly, small group behaviour. The method Weber (1949) chose to achieve generalisations about history was to create constructs which he called 'ideal types':

An . . . ideal type is formed by the one-sided accentuation of one or more points of view and by the synthesis of a great many diffuse, discrete, more or less present and occasionally absent concrete individual phenomena which are arranged according to those one-sided emphasised viewpoints into a unified analytical construct (p. 60).

Many different ideal types could be constructed for each historical event, although Weber believed, but never demonstrated, that the number was limited. Using an ideal type it was possible to have, as it were, experiments in the mind. For example the ideal type of western capitalism could be compared with other economic systems to see in what way they differed from the ideal type. Weber thus brought the sociological study of history down from the search for historical laws to the lower level of a search for explanations of specific historical events. Kahn's scenarios are a good example of the type of explanations Weber sought. Kahn's canonical variations of 'more integrated', 'more inward-looking' and 'greater disarray' are ideal types with which the implications of actions can be studied. The ideal type does not provide a solution to the problem of studying history however. Each ideal type, like each historical law, is determined by the values of the observer and is therefore arbitrary, just as each historical law is arbitrary.

SUMMARY

The comparative method, the search for historical laws, was the dominant method in sociology in the nineteenth century. Each of the major users of the method, Comte, Marx, Spencer and Sorokin, produced different laws from studying the same history. Max Weber pointed out that the difficulty of studying history scientifically lay in the uniqueness of historical events. He attempted to avoid this problem by the use of 'ideal types'—typical constellations of actions and/or thoughts that although related to reality were not derived from reality. These are as arbitrary as the historical laws produced by other theorists. A more quantitative and limited study of history, which remains in the same tradition as the original comparative method in its desire to predict the future in order to control it, was initiated by Ogburn and is carried on today by Kahn and many other writers who receive government and business backing for their studies.

Measurement and analysis 6

Facts, according to my ideas, are merely the elements of truths, and not the truths themselves; of all matters there are none so utterly useless by themselves as your mere matters of fact. A fact, so long as it remains an isolated fact, is a dull, dead, uniformed thing; no object nor event by itself can possibly give us any knowledge, we must compare it with some other, even to distinguish it; and it is the distinctive quality thus developed that constitutes the essence of a thing. . . . To give the least mental value to facts, therefore, we must generalize them, that is to say, we must contemplate them in connexion with other facts, and so discover their agreements and differences, their antecedents, concomitants and consequences. It is true we may frame erroneous and defective theories in so doing . . . nevertheless, if theory may occasionally teach us wrongly, facts without theory or generalization cannot possibly teach us at all.

Mayhew (1851, iv, 1–2)

This penultimate chapter is concerned with detail: the detail of analysis and measurement. The previous chapters have looked at how social 'facts' are collected by experiment, survey, participant observation and the comparative method. Although each of these methods contains, or should contain when used properly, means of distinguishing and measuring social facts and means of demonstrating the relationships between these facts it is possible to abstract this measurement and analysis and consider it separately. This is the purpose of this chapter. In the first part of the chapter four specific types of measurement problems will be studied and their historical development traced: the measurement of attitudes, the measurement of social class, the measurement of documents (which can be classed as a research method itself, like the survey or the experiment) and sociometry. The second part of the chapter will deal with methods of demonstrating relationships between variables. Firstly the developments in the methods of showing the association between variables will be traced and then attempts at prediction, often called the goal of any science, will be discussed.

MEASUREMENT

Measurement is a theoretical problem; for the problem of measurement is that of classifying and ordering reality. How one orders reality is a theoretical question. The simplest measurement problem is to decide whether or not a piece of observed reality does or does not interest the sociologist. What is, or is not, of interest to a sociologist is of course a key theoretical question basic to the discipline. More difficult measurement problems are also ultimately theoretical problems. If a sociologist seeks to construct a scale in which some aspects of reality score higher than others, for example an attitude scale, then he is in fact suggesting a theory of social reality which sees reality as an hierarchical order. Underlying all measurement systems therefore are theoretical assumptions about the nature of social reality.

Attitude scales
Attitude scales are possibly the most widely used scales in sociology. A consideration of their historical development reveals the theoretical assumptions underlying their use. The concept of attitude as a sociological concept was first brought to prominence in Thomas and Znaniecki's work (1927) where they saw attitudes as the 'subjective characteristics of the members of a social group' and distinguished them from social values which were the 'objective cultural elements of social life' (p. 20). This conception of attitude as a 'process of individual consciousness which determines real or possible activity of the individual in the social world' (p. 22), or as a later writer phrased it 'a predisposition to act', remains the theoretical basis for the sociological concept of attitude. The

first measurement of attitude came, however, from a different source and was not conceived of as a measurement of attitude at all but a measurement of social distance.

Robert Park had obtained the idea of social distance from Simmel, under whom he had studied in Germany. When he was engaged in a race relations survey on the West Coast of the United States (1924) he suggested to Bogardus, a co-worker, that the concept might be useful in understanding race prejudice. With this guidance Bogardus went on to create the first attitude scale. The scale measured the attitudes of prejudice by asking people a series of questions about other nationalities, e.g. would they let their daughter marry a Negro, would they let a Negro live next door, would they let a Negro into the country. The important point about these questions was that they were a scale, i.e. if a person answered no to the last question (would he let a Negro into the country) he would almost certainly answer no to the preceding question (would he let a Negro marry his daughter). The Bogardus social distance scale was a significant event in the measurement of attitudes. Park (1924, p. 204) had said that 'it is important not merely to state the opinion, but to indicate also the intensity with which it is held', and this scale achieved that.

In 1927, a year before Bogardus had published his scale, another researcher, Thurstone, had developed a method of scaling that was to be named after him. Thurstone was a psychologist rather than a sociologist. In psychology by 1927 there was already a strong tradition of psychometrics (the construction of scales to measure mental attributes) which is perhaps most famous for the work of Alfred Binet, the father of intelligence tests. Thurstone drew on this tradition to create a new method of scaling. The method comprises giving a series of statements about, say, Negroes to a group of judges. They are each asked independently to rank the statements with regard to their favourableness or unfavourableness to Negroes. Those statements on which the judges agree as to their position along a continuum from favourable to unfavourable become items in the scale. The result of this procedure is a scale with equal appearing intervals between items.

In 1932 a simpler method of scaling was put forward by Likert, an agricultural statistician. Likert's method has the advantage not only of simplicity but also of demonstrating the intensity of an attitude as well as its direction. His method consists of finding two groups of people you already know are poles apart in their attitudes to a topic. These two groups are then given a set of statements relating to the topic, with which they can strongly agree, agree, through to strongly disagree. The statements which are finally used in the scale are those that discriminate between the two groups and correlate highly with all other statements in the scale.

With these two methods at their disposal researchers in the 1930s had a phase of what can only be called attitude scale mania. They correlated attitudes with each other on almost every subject they could think of, often regardless of the theoretical assumptions that underlie the scales. Often, in fact, they had no theory at all. It was not until the Second World War that this measurement mania came to an end and it was during the Second World War also that the measurement of attitudes was taken further. During the war a group of sociologists and other behavioural scientists were brought together under the direction of Samuel Stouffer to conduct studies on the American war effort and in particular upon the American Army. This Research Branch, as it was called, began a new phase in attitude measurement. As they said in their book on the subject published after the war (1950):

> Most of that [Thurstone's] work represented an effort to apply quantitative methods to qualitative data ... the one thing which these chapters have in common, differentiating them from the prewar work, is their effort to treat qualitative data *as* qualitative, not quantitative (p. 4).

The researchers were fully aware that they were putting forward theoretical models when they developed measurement teachniques:

> The objective of much of the Research Branch methodological endeavors ... is to deal *with theoretical models of ordered structures or scales and with technical procedures for testing the applicability of a particular model to a particular set of qualitative data* (p. 3).

The two models and techniques they developed were the scalogram model of Guttman and the latent structure model of Lazarsfeld:

> The scalogram hypothesis is that the items (in the scale) have an order such that, ideally, *persons who answer a given question favourably all have higher ranks on the scale than persons who answer the same question unfavorably* (p. 9).

(Bogardus's scale, mentioned earlier, is a Guttman type scale in this respect):

> The latent structure approach is a generalization of Spearman-Thurstone factor analysis. The basic postulate is that there exists a set of *latent classes, such that the manifest relationship between any two or more items on a questionnaire can be accounted for by the existence of these latent classes and these alone.* This implies that any item has two components—one of which is associated with latent classes and one of which is specific to the item. The specific component of any item is assumed to be independent of the latent classes and *also independent of the specific component of any other item* (p. 19).

The implication of the latent structure approach is that an item in a questionnaire contains in effect two components. This is most easily demonstrated by an example. Say the item 'all Jews are homosexual' appeared on a questionnaire, designed to measure attitudes to Jews. The item would contain two components—one relating to antisemitism, the other to homosexuality. The function of latent structure analysis is to ensure that items used in a scale will be largely concerned with one attitude and not several. The above item would probably not be used because it would be as likely to tap attitudes relating to homosexuality as it would attitudes relating to antisemitism. At this degree of sophistication the measurement of attitudes has remained since 1945. It is possible using latent structure analysis to create attitude scales that are extremely efficient and discriminating *and* measure only one underlying attitude.

Social class
The measurement of attitudes is a measurement of individuals

rather than society. By adding together the scores of individuals on attitude scales the attitudes of groups can be inferred, but it nevertheless remains as a measurement of individuals. An attempt to measure society directly is apparent in the attempt to measure social class structures. There have been two approaches to the problem of constructing measurements of social class. Those making use of the first approach have sought to construct an index of social class that has only one item; those using the second have tried to construct indexes that use a large number of items. The use of one item would, for measurement purposes, be preferable. However the concept of social class is complex and there has been much theoretical argument about what it means. The concept entered sociological discussion with Marx, who defined a social class as an aggregate of people in a similar relationship to the means of production (a class in itself) who became a true class only when they acted as a group (a class for itself). Thus the initial formulation of the concept already contained two different empirical referents for the term.

The theoretical argument became more complex when Weber pointed out that there were three types of social differentiation in society: class, status and power, and that these three were not necessarily coterminous as Marx had presumed. With the introduction of the concept of status Weber made the measurement of class a much more difficult problem, for the status of a group may or may not be related to its economic position. Those who constructed the first measurements of social class were not however sociologists but economists and administrators. Both in England and in America those responsible for analysing census data, the Registrar General and the Bureau of the Census respectively, were among the first to attempt to construct measures of social class. These measures were the creation of categories that appeared to be reasonable to the census staff. Census data refer largely to economic categories so it was the occupations of individuals that were categorised. Crude though this division was it still remains a useful classification to which other variables such as illness, childbirth, death, education and many other important variables can be related. Occupation has remained the most widely used indicator of social class throughout this century. The original class categories have been slightly modified by later researchers who have tried to create a more 'objective' basis for classification by asking samples of the population to rank occupations to produce an agreed measure of what has come to be called 'socio-economic status'.

In 1950 Hatt demonstrated, using Guttman's technique, that the socio-economic scales so produced were in fact a composite of eight different true scales each relating to a group of occupations: political, professional, business, recreation, military, agriculture, manual work and service occupations, i.e. that people could only rank meaningfully within each one of those groups. Although occupation has remained the most important single index of social class other researchers have looked at other variables such as education, race and income. In fact, as early as 1895, Engels suggested that the income of a family could be measured by a standard unit (which he called a 'quet', after Quetelet) which equalled the average consumption of an infant. The disparity of position given by the various indices of socio-economic status has been used in a theory of social behaviour which suggests that the disparity between positions for an individual may lead him to action to achieve a parity (see Lenski, 1954).

More often, however, when several indices conflict an attempt is made to treat each as one of several variables that indicate a person's social class. Such multiple item indicators usually do not include occupation but concentrate instead upon the possessions of those studied. Early studies in this area looked at the amenities and physical condition of houses (Commons, 1908) and the furnishing of rooms in a house (Perry, 1913). Later researchers, tried to be rigorous in the use of such scales. Chapin (1928), for example, measured an individual's social class by his income, his participation in voluntary associations and his possessions, and then correlated each measure with all the others. He found that the measurement of possessions, in terms of what a person owned and how well it was kept, correlated highly with the other two measures and so put it forward as an index of social class.

One of the most interesting attempts to construct a multiple item index that did not use material possessions was that undertaken by Warner (Warner and Lunt, 1941). In his study of 'Yankeetown' Warner had expected to be able to classify social classes by their wealth and occupation. He found however that a classification using just these two items led to anomalies, e.g. he had some people of high wealth and high occupation who were not ranked as top citizens by fellow members of Yankeetown. In his attempt to understand these anomalies he gained from his informants the idea that certain areas of Yankeetown were good socially and certain areas were bad. Using this knowledge he was able to divide the population of Yankeetown into six classes. Individuals were more exactly placed in a particular class by the clubs they belonged to and the evaluation of others as to whether they did or did not belong in a certain social group. Warner was able in this manner to identify social classes by their interaction. He thus defined a social class in terms of its behaviour rather than looking at indices of its behaviour as previous researchers had done.

The measurement of social class remains a difficult problem in sociology. Neither the work of Hatt on socio-economic status nor the work of Warner on interaction in a community fully meets all the theoretical problems raised by the concept of class. New measures of class are continually being created to satisfy the different theoretical perspectives that exist in sociology and no doubt new measures will continue to be created so long as there are competing theoretical perspectives in sociology.

Measurement of documents
The measurement of documents is a research method (comparable to the experiment and the survey), a method of measurement and a method of analysis. However, it seemed appropriate to discuss it under the heading of measurement techniques because it demonstrates clearly the relationship between theory and measurement. Documentary analysis in a quantifiable form, known as 'content

analysis', started at the turn of the century, and as in so many other areas Ogburn was an early pioneer. In 1908 he published a content analysis of child labour laws and was sophisticated enough to realise that the categories into which he classified his data determined his results, i.e. that the variables he considered theoretically important were the ones he used to classify his data thus ensuring that his results would be given in terms of his theoretical categories. The method was further developed by Willey (1926) who wished to determine the impact of the press on public opinion. He argued that it is impossible to see how a news item affects people and therefore the only way to study newspapers is to look at how much of each category of news they print and presume the quantity affects their opinions. Like Ogburn he fully realised that the categories he chose for analysis determined his results and he laid down rules for the determination of categories:

> *The three essentials in classification.* In constructing any system of categories for use in classifying newspaper content three factors must be kept in mind:
> 1. The system of categories must be applicable to all general newspapers.
> 2. It must be so constructed that it will be possible to make comparisons between different papers of the same date, the same papers at different times, or different papers at different times.
> 3. It must give a maximum of precision and reduce the subjective element to a minimum (p. 32).

Content analysis took a new turn in the work of the Hawthorne researchers. In their analysis of interviews they developed a method of content analysis which took account not only of the frequencies with which topics were mentioned but also took account of the attitude of workers towards those topics. The frequency, or what they called the 'urgency', of a topic was calculated by the ratio of comments per 100 interviews. The attitude, or what they called the 'tone', of a topic was calculated by the ratio of favourable to unfavourable comments per 100 workers. Using this method content analysis becomes more than enumeration. The method used at Hawthorne has been superseded by another method, related to content analysis, which seeks to find the attitudes of individuals or institutions. This method, known as 'contingency analysis', presumes that if two items are next to each other they have a relationship to each other. In this way, it is argued, it is possible to understand the implicit assumptions about the world that were in the mind of the writer, even if the writer himself was not aware of them, e.g. a continuous association of 'Ford motor cars' and 'freedom' was found in the production of one commercial radio station which had a Ford franchise. Contingency and content analysis were used with great sophistication during the Second World War by the American Army (see Laswell, 1942) to analyse the speeches of enemies and thus predict their behaviour. The effectiveness of the method remains dependent on the effectiveness of the theory that guides its choice of categories and this is true of all methods of measurement.

Sociometry
Sociometry is a specific research technique developed by a Romanian psychiatrist, Jacob Moreno, for therapeutic purposes. It has been extensively used by sociologists for non-therapeutic ends, purely as a technique for measuring the structure of groups. Individuals are asked a question about who they would like to live with or work with or sit next to. In Moreno's use of the technique the people concerned were allowed to carry out their choice, as far as possible. He considered that without the respondent knowing that his choice would be 'real' the technique was invalid. This has not prevented later researchers from using it extensively without carrying out their respondents' choices. The responses of individuals are plotted as a 'sociogram' (or more recently in a matrix) in which each individual is represented by a circle, and his choice, or rejection, is shown by lines to other individuals.

The technique is valuable because it is easy to administer and analyse, and gives at a glance a picture of a group's structure. However, it has been demonstrated that just as in content analysis different categories produce different answers so in sociometry different questions produce different structures. This is not a major criticism but emphasises once again the relationship between theory and measurement. The choice of questions has to be guided by a theoretical proposition, or propositions, before the answers can be used to look at the structure of a group, for different structures are derived from different theories.

ANALYSIS

The problem that faces any research worker when he has measured and collected his variables is to show how the variables relate one to another. This is the problem of analysis. Just as measurement is basically a theoretical problem so is analysis. The search for relationships should be guided by a theory that suggests why some variables should be related to each other and also, as a corollary, suggests why others should not. The problem of analysis then is a theoretical problem and its use is best exemplified in the works of one of the greatest sociological theorists: Emile Durkheim.

Durkheim developed sociological analysis as a method of testing and improving theory, in *Suicide* which was published in 1897. This work is recognised as a classic of sociological literature. In his analysis of suicide statistics, which forms the focus of the book, Durkheim recognised and solved many of the basic problems of sociological analysis. The method adopted by Durkheim may best be described as 'proposition testing': a proposition, or hypothesis, is put forward as a plausible explanation for an association between two variables, e.g. it is proposed that marriage and suicide are related. This association is teased out in detail by holding other variables, such as age, constant. The same association between the two variables is shown to exist in different countries and at different times, thus demonstrating that the association is not spurious. While demonstrating this association several alternative explanations for the relationship are considered and all are rejected because they are not in accord with the facts. In this way one theoretical proposition is finally shown to be the only explanation of the relationship discovered. A typical analysis of this type is contained in the second chapter concerning egoistic suicide (book 2, chapter 3) and a brief account of the argument of part of this chapter is given here to illustrate the method.

Absolute figures of suicides show that unmarried persons commit suicide less than married persons in France. However the unmarried total includes children under sixteen years of age which distorts the figures. If these children are removed from the unmarried total the disparity between the suicides of the unmarried and the married is lessened. This result still gives a false picture however, for the majority of the unmarried age group are under 25 years of age whereas married people are mainly between 40 and 45 years of age. Older people commit suicide half as often again as younger people if age is the only variable taken into account. But married older people commit suicide perceptibly less than that, so although the raw data show that unmarried people commit suicide less than married, when age is taken into account the relationship is reversed. This is true of Italy, Wurtemberg and Prussia as well as France. This can be shown more clearly by calculating a suicide rate for each age and social group.

> Under such conditions one may, for example, compare unmarried persons of from 25 to 30 years with married and widowed persons of the same age . . . the influence of marital status will thus be isolated from all other influences and all its possible variations will appear (1952 edition, p. 175).

Durkheim then goes on to calculate suicide rates for different groups. Having accomplished this he considers two propositions explaining the relationships he has demonstrated. The first is that it is the stabilising influence of a family that reduces the suicide rate of married people. The second is that the fittest people in the population, i.e. the ones least likely to commit suicide, select each other as marriage partners. He discounts the second argument in several ways pointing out for example that young married people, below 20 years of age, are more likely to commit suicide than young unmarried people which would not be true if selection were the explanation. He finds further support for the first proposition by demonstrating that married couples with children are less likely to commit suicide than childless married couples.

In arguments such as the one given above Durkheim developed a method of analysis which meets many of the problems of sociology. The analysis is multivariate. Each additional variable is brought in, in turn, further to explicate relationships already studied. This develops what is known today as 'contextual analysis' where the relationship between two variables is 'elaborated' by the introduction of a third. This elaboration can take three forms— 'explanation', 'interpretation' and 'specification'. In the example given above Durkheim attempts to 'explain' the relationship between suicide and marriage. He finds it is not due to national peculiarities or selection at marriage. He therefore seeks an 'interpretation' that explains the relationship and finds it in the solidarity of family life. Finally he 'specifies' the conditions under which the relationship holds. Thus he points out, for example, that relative advantage of marriage varies from country to country although it always remains an advantage to be married (i.e. married people always commit suicide less than unmarried people of the same age).

As well as being multivariate the analysis is also replicative, i.e. the same variables are studied in different situations, time and time again. This has two advantages. First, it lends greater credence to the existence of the relationship. Second, by looking at smaller and smaller units Durkheim sought to avoid the 'aggregative fallacy'. This fallacy is common in sociological analysis. Basically it consists of interpreting relationships between groups of data as though they are relationships between units. A simple example demonstrates the problem: if there are two groups of people each with different suicide rates, those 15–25, and those 25–40 years of age, then simple interpretation of these rates would suggest that married people under 25 are more likely to commit suicide than those not married, whereas between 25 and 40 the reverse is the case:

Age	Unmarried	Married
15–25	350	597
25–40	1021	348

This would however be an error. The true picture is that those who marry under 20 are more likely to commit suicide:

Age	Unmarried	Married
15–20	113	500
20–25	237	97
25–30	394	122
30–40	627	226

(Tables adapted from Durkheim, 1952 edn, Table XXI, p. 178. France (1889–91), suicides committed per 1 million inhabitants of each age and marital status group, average year.)

By aggregating the 15–20 and 20–25 age classes a false impression can be given. The smaller the unit a researcher studies, the less likely he is to commit this fallacy.

Durkheim demonstrated this method of analysis in 1897. By 1928 statistical tools had been developed and used that made the method much more exact. At the time Durkheim wrote *Suicide* the 'correlation coefficient' had already been developed by Galton and Pearson. This is a way of expressing mathematically the degree of association between two variables in a simple way. If two variables are in perfect association the correlation coefficient will be 1, if they are inversely related it will be –1 and if there is no relationship it will be 0. In 1920 T. J. Woofter in a study of Negro migration in the cotton belt used Pearson's correlations to demonstrate that the migration was associated with lack of agricultural opportunity: the correlation between the number of Negroes in an area and the number of independent Negro farmers was 0.8, whereas the correlation between the number of Negroes in an area and the number of Negro labourers was only 0.2.

In 1924 Stuart Rice further developed the use of correlation techniques. Trained at Columbia like Ogburn, who also made a contribution that will be discussed later, Rice made many small contributions to the use of statistics in sociology. His particular contribution to the analysis of association was in the use of rank correlations. It is not always possible in sociology to assign real numbers to variables but it is often possible to put them in some sort of order or rank. Rice was the first to demonstrate in sociology that these ranks could be correlated, when he showed that there was an association between the size of a town and Republican voting. He ranked towns by size and ranked them also by the number of Republican voters. He then calculated a rank correlation coefficient to demonstrate the association between town size and voting for the Republican party.

The most important contribution to the mechanics of analysis was made by Ogburn. In 1928 he demonstrated the use of partial correlation coefficients. These are correlation coefficients calculated while holding constant all other variables except the ones under study. They thus give an exactitude to the method developed by Durkheim. Ogburn correlated five variables with votes for Smith, the Democratic Party nominee for President of the USA: the percentage of foreign-born people in the population, the percentage of urban dwellers, the percentage of Catholics (Smith was a Catholic), the percentage voting for the repeal of prohibition, and the percentage normally voting Democratic. The correlations between voting for Smith and each of the variables were 0.33 foreign born, 0.33 urban dwellers, 0.47 Catholics, 0.65 repeal of prohibition and 0.11 Democratic. However Ogburn realised that the variables were related, e.g. urban voters tend to be more opposed to prohibition and are also likely to be Democrats and Catholics. He therefore calculated partial correlation coefficients. When this was done the urban vote was shown to be *inversely* related to voting for Smith, —0.18. The apparent urban support was due to the fact that urban voters were Catholic, Democratic and supporters of the repeal of prohibition. This technique of partial correlation is a sophisticated and rapid way of carrying out the same kind of analysis as that developed by Durkheim.

Partial correlations are not the end of the development of analytic techniques. Complex mathematical techniques have proceeded much farther with the development of factor analysis and latent structure analysis. This progress has been made possible by the use of electronic computers. But the principle and purpose of these methods remains the same as the principle and purpose of Durkheim's analysis—the teasing out of the relationships between variables by controlling those variables. They need not be considered here. What I would like to consider is a development parallel to that of statistical techniques: prediction. Once an association between variables is demonstrated it is possible to use that relationship to predict. This fact has been used in the field of criminology with great success from its early beginnings in 1923. With prediction, sociology fulfils the dreams of Comte who wished to see sociology used for social engineering.

The methods for predicting individual behaviour, using demonstrated relationships between sociological variables as a guide, were pioneered by S. B. Warner in 1923 in a study of the factors associated with successful parole from prison. It is in the works of Burgess, the man who has already been mentioned as a pioneer in the field of urban ecology, and in the works of the Gluecks that the methods were fully developed. Burgess, in collaboration with others (1928), studied the variables associated with success or failure of 3000 paroled prisoners in Illinois. He looked at twenty-one variables which were in turn subdivided into a number of categories, e.g. type of offence was subdivided into seven categories including murder, robbery, fraud, etc. He then compared the average rate of parole violation with the parole violation of paroled prisoners having a particular factor. Thus he discovered that in one prison the average rate of parole violation was 28 per cent whereas 42 per cent of prisoners who were convicted of fraud violated their parole. Burgess assigned a score of one to each factor: every time a factor possessed by a prisoner was below the average violation rate for the prison he scored one (if it was above the average rate it was ignored). When this was done it was possible to work out 'expectancy rates' for violation of parole. Prisoners with 16 to 21 points could be expected to violate their parole in only 1.5 per cent of cases whereas prisoners with only 2 to 4 points would be expected to violate their parole in 76 per cent of cases.

One of the criticisms levelled at Burgess's system was that it gave equal weight to each variable whereas it was obvious that some variables were better predictors than others. This criticism was met in the work of the Gluecks, a husband and wife team, who, working independently of Burgess, produced their own prediction tables for parole violation in 1930. Sheldon Glueck was by training a lawyer. His wife Eleanor was a social worker, and his brother was a psychiatrist. Together he and his wife made a formidable research team. Like Burgess they became involved in the practical problems of parole. Their methods were, however, much more detailed and rigorous than Burgess's. They checked the information given in the official files about the prisoners and, in the majority of cases, interviewed the ex-prisoners they were studying or a close relative. They even checked the identity of the men they were studying, using fingerprints. As well as these more extensive checks on their information they also carried out more extensive analysis than Burgess. They looked at fifty variables they considered might be related to parole violation. Most important, by the use of statistical techniques, they were able to isolate and assign weights to the six most important variables. They found that the most important variable associated with parole violation was previous work habits: poor work habits correlated 0.42 with parole violation. Also of importance was the seriousness and frequency of previous crimes, arrests, and penal experience; and economic responsibility and mental abnormality.

It is not, however, for these studies that the Gluecks are primarily remembered. Their major importance lies in their later studies into the variables associated with juvenile delinquency, in which they used methods similar to those they had developed in their studies of parole violation. The importance of these studies, the first of which was published in 1939, lies in the attempt to find causal explanations of delinquency. It is possible to predict without understanding causes. For example, it is known that there is an association between certain areas of a city and juvenile delinquency. Shaw and McKay suggested this was due to social disorganisation yet Whyte demonstrated that such areas were not disorganised, merely organised in a different pattern to that of middle-class society. Thus Shaw's explanation of cause may be wrong. This does not invalidate any prediction made from Shaw's data about the proportion of delinquents found in any area. To demonstrate causality three things are necessary. First it must be shown that there is an association between two variables—as one varies so does the other; secondly it must be demonstrated that one variable occurs before the other, otherwise it could not cause the other. These two things are not sufficient to demonstrate cause, although both are necessary. The final demonstration of cause is that there should be a theoretical connection between the two variables. This last item lays any explanation of causality open to dispute for different theoretical explanations can be advanced for the same covariation of variables. The Gluecks considered that they had demonstrated causality. They studied two groups of juveniles. One group was known to be delinquent and the other non-delinquent. From their various theories of delinquency they derived certain important variables which they measured. They found that there were significant statistical differences between the delinquents and non-delinquents with regard to some of these variables and that some variables, or groups of variables, were present in the delinquents *only* and that these were present *before* their delinquency. They therefore attributed causal significance to those variables and used them in a prediction table. (see table 2)

With these prediction studies social research methods may be said to have reached at least one of the goals set for sociology by Comte. Sociology can 'see in order to foresee and foresee in order to anticipate'. With the methods also the basic problem of social research has to be faced. If social research is to be scientific it must make causal explanations of behaviour which enable predictions to be made. Predictions can be made in the limited field of criminology but the problem of causal explanations still remains. There is no body of accepted theory within which the different successful predictions can be integrated. Each theory competes with every other theory to explain the same results. A discussion of why this is the case and a consideration of the solutions proffered to the meet problem form the focus of the final chapter.

TABLE 2 *Identification of potential juvenile delinquency based on five social factors*

Score class	Delinquency rate (%)	Non-delinquency rate (%)	Total number of cases
Less than 200	8.2	91.8	293
200–250	37.0	63.0	108
250–300	63.5	36.5	192
300 or over	89.2	10.8	297

Predictive factors	Delinquency scores
DISCIPLINE OF BOY BY FATHER:	
Firm but kindly	9.3
Lax	59.8
Overstrict or erratic	72.5
SUPERVISION OF BOY BY MOTHER:	
Suitable	9.9
Fair	57.5
Unsuitable	83.2
AFFECTION OF FATHER FOR BOY:	
Warm (including overprotective)	33.8
Indifferent or hostile	75.9
AFFECTION OF MOTHER FOR BOY:	
Warm (including overprotective)	43.1
Indifferent or hostile	86.2
COHESIVENESS OF FAMILY:	
Marked	20.6
Some	61.3
None	96.9

Source: Glueck and Glueck (1950), Table xx–3, pp. 261, 262.

SUMMARY

Measurement and analysis are not merely technical problems but fundamental theoretical problems. Four measurement problems: the measurement of attitudes, the measurement of social class, the measurement of documents and sociometric measurements were studied and each was shown to be concerned with theoretical problems. An examination of the methods of analysis used by Durkheim and developed quantitatively by Woofter, Rice and Ogburn came to the same conclusion. Prediction studies were shown to face theoretical problems in an acute form because of their expressed concern with causality.

Woe to the doctoral candidate who dared question the union of objectivity with neutrality.

R.W. Friedrichs (1970, p. 81)

There was a great danger in the esoteric existence of the specialist, a fatal fascination in the backstage intimacy of the puppet-theatre. After a while you lapsed into a subtle contempt for the happy ignorance of the herd . . .

The mother tongue became strange to you and you ended perched like a stylite on a pillar, surveying a desert and wondering where the people had gone.

Morris West (1968, p. 274)

Sociology began as an attempt to change the world, an attempt to control the social changes which were occurring at the turn of the eighteenth century. This control was to be achieved by the methods of science. Science was to give men both the understanding of their social world and the means to control it. Science was the tool of sociology not the essence of sociology. This concern with the control of society formed the main theme underlying the comparative method and all the various developments of the survey method. Men felt compassion for the poor and the weak and sought to help them. However the tool—the scientific method—began to determine sociological aims. Sociology became identified with the scientific study of society and any study that was not 'scientific' became dismissed as non-sociological. This in itself was not necessarily harmful; what was harmful was that the model of science that sociologists adopted and emulated was the nineteenth-century positivist model. This perceived science not as a particular belief system but as a method which enabled one to find objective reality. The scientific method itself was perceived to be free of any beliefs or values and the use of it enabled one to find truth in the absolute sense of the word. This model of science implied that the sociologist should not bring in his values into the search for an understanding of society, and sociologists therefore sought to attain a nirvana known as 'value-neutrality' in their empirical work. One of the ironies of this commitment to a value-free scientific sociology was that it achieved its greatest acceptance in the 1950s, at the very time when physical scientists were beginning to abandon their commitment to a value-neutral science. Tied up with the pre-eminence of the scientific method in sociology was a theoretical position derived in large measure from biology. This position viewed society as an organism, a system of interconnected parts. (Spencer took this viewpoint, Shaw derived his theoretical position from biology, and Parsons was trained as a biologist.)

This view of society as an organism or system fitted in well with the conception of sociology as a science. The task of a scientific sociology became that of finding out what were the units in the organism and how they related to each other, in fact to understand how the organism functioned and what maintained it as a system. Such a task implied a distancing from the details of social life. Social life was 'abstracted' into 'theoretical concepts' which were then 'operationalised' and the relationships between the concepts studied. This view of the social world enabled sociologists to believe that they were value-free and laid stress on the way men's lives were influenced by social currents which it was assumed were beyond their control. The result was that sociology became concerned with fitting man into his social environment—with adjusting him to his work, for example. A far cry from the early sociologists' dreams of using science as a means whereby rational men could control their social world.

Now, however, the view of sociology as a science, in the simplistic sense that science was viewed by many sociologists, is crumbling, if it has not already fallen. The pressures for its collapse came from three fronts. First, it became increasingly obvious that the realities of social research did not accord with the positivist model of science put forward. Second, philosophers and historians of science began to demonstrate that the model of science adopted by sociologists was a false model of the natural sciences. Third, there remained within sociology a group of theorists, deriving their inspiration from Weber and Marx, who always insisted that sociology could not be a science like the physical sciences because of the very nature of its subject matter—man.

The discontinuity between the model of a scientific sociology and the actual practice of sociological research was most obvious when the experimental method of investigation was used. It was clear that the process of measurement affected the variables measured—the so-called 'Hawthorne effect'. Apologists for the model of sociology as a science were quick to point out that this was true in atomic physics also. Pointing out that sociologists have strange bedfellows did not solve the problem. (The dilemmas faced by atomic physicists were incidentally one of the reasons for the reappraisal of what constituted a science that was undertaken by scientists and philosophers of science.) The lack of fit between sociology and a positivist science became most obvious when the conception of value neutrality in sociology was attacked. It is impossible for sociology to be neutral in respect of social values. Myrdal (1955) was the first to face up to this problem in an empirical work, in his study of the American Negro, but his answer of stating values before going on to conduct research in a kind of catharsis, was a palliative rather than a solution. (The Webbs (1932) had discussed the problem in general terms suggesting that the sociologist should deliberately seek evidence to refute his assumptions but they did not demonstrate its use in an empirical work.)

The potential universe of observations is infinite and in choosing a problem to study the sociologist is swayed by his values. The concepts he chooses to use limit his perception of the world and channel it in certain directions and the same is true of the propositions that contain those concepts. The rules of interpretation a sociologist uses are not self-evident but form part of a philosophical system which has implicit assumptions. Different types of logical interpretations—Aristotelian or Dialectic for example—produce different results. The proof of a proposition is always a matter of judgment. One can never be absolutely certain that a proposition is validated and the choice of when to accept a proposition as proven lies with the sociologist. It is no answer to these criticisms to insist that mathematics and statistics are value-free because they are themselves philosophical systems. A commitment to only accept results that are statistically significant is a commitment to the assumption that statistical significance is equivalent to substantive significance and a commitment to a view of the social world as probabilistic rather than deterministic or random. The acceptance of the myth of a value-neutral science of sociology has had serious consequences for sociology as a discipline. It has first of all led to a selection of problems for study not because of their interest but because the techniques were available to deal with them. As Peter Berger (1963, p. 13) says, 'in science as in love a concentration on technique is quite likely to lead to impotence', and this seems to have been the situation in sociology. Training in demography declined just as overpopulation became recognised as a problem. It has also meant an abdication of responsibility by sociologists. Giving up their right to choose fields of study in the attempt to be value-neutral has led them to have their fields of study chosen by others who were not so squeamish. Thus the American military, American business and the CIA chose for the sociologist what he was to study by providing him with money to pursue study in certain fields. The most blatant example of this was Project Camelot, a study financed by the American army into the possibility of predicting revolutions in Latin America, which could of course be used by them to forestall such revolutions. This project finally collapsed in a storm of protest but many sociologists were willing to take part in it, tempted by the huge research grants offered and salving their consciences with the stance of a value-neutral sociology.

The idea that science is free of values is a chimera. Science ultimately rests on a commitment to efficient prediction. This implies firstly that only evidence which can be observed and identified by more than one person can be accepted as empirical. Secondly it implies that such empirical evidence must be recurrent so that it can be observed again and again. Thirdly it implies that there is an order to the universe—a pattern to the relations observed between items of empirical evidence. Not one of these three implications is a self-evident truth. To believe in an underlying order waiting to be discovered is an act of faith as great as a belief in a god. The scientist commits himself to a belief system just as any other believer commits himself to a religious or philosophical faith and as in any religious faith he is sustained by his fellow believers. The supposed value-neutrality of the scientist is nothing more than a commitment to submit to the judgment of others his view of the world. When other scientists agree with his perception of empirical reality he is said to have proved a proposition or hypothesis or theory. The attempt to separate out a pure and applied science, whether in the natural or the social sciences, is an act of selfishness. A pure scientist in his work is salving his itch for knowledge. This is not a commendable value-free dedication but an act of selfishness. The idea of a positive science of sociology is nothing more than an attempt to fit sociology to an outdated model of science.

The third pressure to abandon the stance of a value-free scientific sociology has come from within the sociological tradition itself. Both Marx and Weber saw the social world not as something 'out there', separate from man, but as something that was at one and the same time both external to man and yet contained within him. Marx called this interaction between the individual and his social and material world 'the dialectic'. The dialectic expresses the fundamental duality of social life—that men create their society and yet are constrained by their creation. A related distinction was made by Weber when he distinguished between the social and natural sciences. He insisted that sociology could never be like the natural sciences because the objects of its study were themselves aware—men had explanations for their actions. Any sociological explanation would therefore have to be on two levels. The first level would be concerned with showing the patterned regularities in men's actions just as a natural scientist would show patterned regularities in the movement of particles. This he called 'causal explanation'. The second level would have to explain the motives underlying these actions. This he called 'explanation on the level of meaning'.

These ideas have been further developed in recent years under numerous headings such as 'action theory', 'phenomenology', 'symbolic interactionism' and 'ethnomethodology', all of which subtly differ but all of which insist upon the importance of appreciating the dynamic duality inherent in the social world between man's perception of his world and the world's pressure upon him. The importance of this dialectical relationship is that it insists that sociology can never be a science. A sociological prediction can never be successful because it enters men's consciousness and they are then free to change their behaviour to invalidate the prediction. The most elegant statement of this paradox was given by Seeley (1963) who postulated three theorems:

1. that social science is action: whatever a sociologist does he intervenes in the processes of the social world;
2. inexhaustibility: one can never exhaust the social world because in describing it one adds to it;
3. freedom: every theory enters into social behaviour and in such a way that men are free to change their behaviour to negate it.

The consequence of these three theorems is that sociology will never be presented with recurrent patterns, a fundamental necessity for scientific prediction.

These philosophical shifts in the orientation of sociology can be related to its historical growth. From its early beginnings until the 1930s sociology remained in what Friedrichs (1970) calls the prophetic stance. It sought to understand the world in order to be able to change it. This was the essence of the comparative method.

It was also the underlying motivation of the proponents of the social survey as a research method. It was adopted because it was a way of convincing administrators of the need for change. The concern of sociology was humanitarian—65 per cent of doctorate theses in the period 1920–24, for example, were about social problems. During the 1930s another strand in sociological thought began to emerge and ultimately dominated sociology in the 1950s. This was the detached curiosity of the scientist exemplified most clearly in the use of the experiment in social psychology and the use of statistics in sociology. The search for data to convince administrators of the need for change became a search for data for its own sake. The best workers of the period, Ogburn and Lewin for example, were able to espouse a science of society and yet select a problem because of its intrinsic interest rather than its amenability to the use of developed techniques. But many began to select problems because they were measurable rather than because they were interesting—a process that culminates in a type of serious (?) study of children's literature (Child *et al.*, 1946) which has statements such as:

> Because of the low incidence of fairies as central or anti-social characters, no detailed comparison with the other types of character can be made. ... The most striking fact is the extremely high incidence of aggression, which among fairies is not only the most frequent category of behavior, but occurs almost three times as often as the next most frequent one (p. 52).

What were the pressures leading sociologists to adopt a value-neutral scientific stance and why has that stance recently collapsed with a rebirth of prophetic sociology concerned with changing society as well as understanding it? The pressures towards thinking of sociology as scientific rather than artistic came from a desire to have the findings of sociology on social problems accepted by all sections of society. If sociologists wanted to change the world they first had to persuade others to accept their definitions of what the social world was really like. To achieve this they needed some sort of legitimation for their pronouncements on family life and crime other than already established polemical positions. They found this legitimation in science. As Bendix (1961) says: 'In their eagerness to make the social sciences more scientific, social scientists persuade others and themselves that human advancement is identical with the advancement of scientific knowledge—*their* scientific knowledge' (p. 35).

The lure of believing they were the possessors of the only true explanation of the social world may also have played its part. Knowledge not possessed by others is always seductive in the possibilities it gives of demonstrating your cleverness and of having power over others. While knowledge of social life remains at the level of good journalism it does not give this aura but once call such knowledge 'scientific' and it becomes esoteric and important.

Other influences were also at work, connected with the success of sociology as a university subject. The findings of sociology were easily dismissed either as statements of the obvious or as expressions of 'do-gooders'. Even today the distinction between sociology and social work is not clear in most people's minds. One way of gaining both academic and general recognition and respect for sociology was to divorce it from its roots in compassion for the poor. Early in the development of sociology a distinction was made between social work and sociology, a distinction made on the basis of recognising sociology as a science. The acceptance of sociology as a value-free science meant also the possibility of research grants from governmental agencies. It was no accident that Ogburn was both the recipient of the first major government research grant and also a man who insisted that sociology could be a value-free science useful to Tory and Communist alike.

The success of sociology in terms of the numbers of graduates and undergraduates it recruited to its banner was also a factor in the rise of the conception of a value-free scientific sociology. Before 1922 half the articles and books produced in the USA on sociology were written by three men: Ogburn, Chapin and Small. These men could be prophets, could advocate change, could make a living in this way. It was not true of the next generation. Between

1920 and 1930 the number of postgraduates increased tremendously and the same growth rate has persisted to the present day—before the first world war there were less than 500 members of the American Sociological Society, by 1928 there were 1,500, by 1938 2,000 and by 1968 6,000 members. A society cannot support so many prophets, so many advocates of change. Nor did the students concerned want to be prophets. Sociology was for them a university subject like any other, and their intention was to find jobs, not to change the world. A value-free sociology enabled them to do this. Their task became not to question the basic assumptions that underlie their society but to create the conditions for the efficient functioning of that society—social engineering rather than social criticism.

If all these factors were operating to lead to a value-free sociology, why has that stance collapsed? The philosophical pressures for its collapse have already been discussed—the realisation that sociology could not be value-free, the realisation that science was not value-free and the theoretical alternative to a conception of sociology as a science—but these pressures must have had their origin, their chance to be effective, because of changes in the position of sociology in society and changes in society. One change was almost certainly the success of sociology, particularly in America, in gaining the status of an established discipline and becoming part of the establishment. Any radical critique of the establishment would have to criticise sociology as part of that establishment. This is what did happen when Civil Rights and Vietnam became issues for students. Another pressure was undoubtedly the lack of a career for sociologists. While a sociology degree in the 'value-free science' gave access to good posts in education and business it was supported by the majority of students. When these job avenues closed, and they have closed in the past five years, the discipline could no longer rely on their support. Unfortunately there is no evidence to support or refute these generalisations and they must therefore remain at the level of speculation.

If sociology cannot be a value-free science but must be

committed to change by the nature of its subject matter, man, then what will be its future? To what will it be committed? There seems little doubt that the methods of the survey, the experiment, participant observation and the comparative method will continue, with perhaps a revival of interest in the comparative method. The use of these methods in future must, however, be more self-conscious. The distinction between observer and observed cannot be one in which the observer 'knows' and the observed is 'ignorant'; this dehumanising effect of a positivist science is thankfully discarded. Both observer and observed have perspectives and interpretations of the world and the perspective of the observer is no more correct than that of the observed. The arrogance of concepts such as 'false consciousness' must be abandoned. If, as sociologists, we wish to agree on an interpretation of the world, that is our privilege, but our interpretation is no more true than any other. It should be clearer than other interpretations, its implications better specified, but it remains an interpretation. If the act of sociological measurement must cause change, let us cause change, in a direction that we believe is good rather than bad. This requires no great revolution in sociological research. Researchers have always tried to mitigate the harmful effects of their research. The difference lies in our attitude to this attempt at mitigation. If we treat sociology as a positive science, then such mitigation is an aberration in the search for predictive efficiency. If however we treat sociology as a discipline—a discipline that like a science offers its methods for criticism by fellow members of the discipline but unlike a science can never study recurrent situations —then the commitment to help rather than harm others can be seen as part of the ethics of the discipline rather than an import grafted on. Sociology grew out of compassion and a desire to change the world. There is no reason why it should not continue to act out of compassion and change the world for the better.

SUMMARY

Sociology emerged as an attempt to control the world using

the methods of science. From 1930 onwards the assumption that the goal of sociology was to become scientific increasingly dominated sociological thought aided by a theoretical position that viewed the social world as an organic system. The model of science that was adopted was a false one and the attempt to change sociology to fit the model led to the false and untenable position of value neutrality. No science, natural or social, can be entirely value free; the natural sciences rely finally on a commitment to a value of predictive efficiency. A commitment by sociologists to the value of predictive efficiency, and only the value of predictive efficiency, implies a freedom to manipulate other men that is morally repugnant. It is not however only morally repugnant. It is also impossible. Men unlike physical objects are aware of the predictions made about their behaviour and can therefore modify that behaviour nullifying or modifying any prediction. Each man, as Kelly said (see Bannister and Fransella, 1972), is an experimenter in the social world. Each social experiment has to recognise that man is both the experimental object and is himself an experimenter. This does not imply however that it is entirely impossible for sociologists to predict other people's behaviour. Each man may be an experimenter but he carries out his experiments within a framework of constraints set up by other men both living and dead. It is these constraints, these social currents that enable sociologists to predict other people's behaviour in most circumstances. However in using these constraints for prediction sociologists make men aware of these constraints on their choices of action and hence they may liberate them from the constraints, thus ultimately invalidating their predictions.

References and further reading

In writing this book numerous books and articles have been examined but it would clutter the narrative to list them all in the text. Many of these books are difficult to obtain and for the undergraduate student unnecessary. I have therefore provided two lists. The first, subdivided by chapters, is for the interested undergraduate who may wish to follow up my ideas further in accessible texts. The second is for the more determined reader and researcher and includes *all* the books and articles I have consulted. This book has still only scratched the surface of its topic and I hope the second list will provide other students with an entrée into a little studied field of sociology.

References in the text are by author's name and date of publication, details being given in the second section of the bibliography.

SECTION I

CHAPTER I. THE ORIGINS OF SOCIOLOGY

Glazer, N. (1959) 'The rise of social research in Europe', in D. Lerner, ed. *The Human Meaning of the Social Sciences*, New York, Meridian.

Dawe, A. (1971) 'The two sociologies' in K. Thompson and J. Tunstall, eds, *Sociological Perspectives*, Penguin Books.

Nisbet, R. (1966) *The Sociological Tradition*, Basic Books.

CHAPTER 2. THE EXPERIMENT

Roethlisberger, F. J. and Dickson, W. J. (1966) *Management and the Worker*, Harvard University Press.

Sherif, M. (1936a) *The Psychology of Social Norms*, Harper & Row.
Lewin, K., Lippitt, R. and White, R. K. (1971) 'Patterns of aggresive behaviour in experimentally created social climates', in D. S. Pugh, ed, *Organization Theory*, Penguin Books.
Bales, R. F. (1951) *Interaction Process Analysis*, Addison Wesley; Landsdowne Press Reprint 1971.

CHAPTER 3. THE SURVEY

Madge, J. (1963) *The Origins of Scientific Sociology*, Tavistock.
Pfautz, H. W. (1967) *Charles Booth on the City*, University of Chicago Press.
Simey, T. S. and Simey, M. B. (1960) *Charles Booth, Social Scientist*, Oxford University Press.
Faris, R. E. L. (1967) *Chicago Sociology 1920–1932*, University of Chicago Press.
Lynd, R. S. and Lynd, H. M. (1929) *Middletown: A Study in Contemporary American Culture*, Harcourt Brace.
Lazarsfeld, P. F., Berelson, B. and Gaudet, H. (1948) *The People's Choice*, Columbia University Press.

CHAPTER 4. PARTICIPANT OBSERVATION AND LIFE HISTORIES

Anderson, N. (1961) *The Hobo*, Chicago, Phoenix Edition.
Thrasher, F. M. (1963) *The Gang*, Chicago, Phoenix Edition.
Whyte, W. F. (1943) *Street Corner Society*, University of Chicago Press.
Shaw, C. R. (1967) *The Jack-Roller*, Chicago, Phoenix Edition.
Becker H. S. (1951) 'The professional dance musician and his audience', *American Journal of Sociology*, vol. 57.

CHAPTER 5. THE COMPARATIVE METHOD

Sklair, L. (1970) *The Sociology of Progress*, Routledge.
Thompson, K. (1972) 'The emergence of sociology', Unit 2 of The Open University Second Level Course, *The Sociological Perspective*, D283.

Mitchell, G. D. (1968) *A Hundred Years of Sociology*, Duckworth.
Kahn, H. and Wiener, J. (1967) *The Year 2000*, Macmillan.

CHAPTER 6. MEASUREMENT AND ANALYSIS

Stouffer, S. A. *et al.* (1950) *Measurement and Prediction: Vol. IV, American Soldier Series*, Princeton University Press.
Warner, W. L. and Lunt, P. S. (1941) *The Social Life of a Modern Community*, Yale University Press.
Pool, I. de Sola, (1959) *Trends in Content Analysis*, University of Illinois Press.
Moreno, J. L. (1934) *Who Shall Survive?*, Washington, D.C., Nervous and Mental Disease Publishing Co.
Durkheim, E. (1951) *Suicide*, trans. and ed. G. Simpson, New York, Free Press.

CHAPTER 7. THE DEVELOPMENT OF SOCIOLOGY

Friedrichs, R. W. (1970) *A Sociology of Sociology*, New York Free Press.

SECTION 2

Anderson, N. (1923/1961) *The Hobo: the sociology of the homeless man*, University of Chicago Press, Phoenix Edition 1961.
Alpert, H. (1963) 'Some observations on the state of sociology', *Pacific Sociological Review*, vol. 6.
Annals of the Royal Statistical Society (1834–1934)
Argyris, C. (1965) *Personality and Organization*, Harper.
Aron, R. (1968) *Main Currents in Sociological Thought*, vol. 1, Penguin Books.
Asch, S. E. (1952) 'Effects of group pressure upon the modification and distortion of judgements', in *Understanding Society*, Open University Press/Macmillan.
Ashton, T. S. (1934) *Economic and Social Investigations in Manchester 1833–93*

Bales, R. F. (1950) 'A set of categories for the analysis of small group interaction', *American Sociological Review*, vol. 15.

Bales, R. F. (1951a) *Interaction Process Analysis*, Addison Wesley, Reading, Mass./Landsdowne Press reprint, 1971.

Bales, R. F. (1955) 'How people interact in conferences', *Scientific American*, March.

Bales, R. F. *et al.* (1951b) 'Channels of communication in small groups', *American Sociological Review*, vol. 16.

Bannister, D. and Fransella, F. (1971) *Inquiring Man*, Penguin Books.

Baritz, L. (1960) *The Servants of Power*, Wesleyan University Press.

Barnes, H. E., ed. (1925) *History and Prospects of the Social Sciences*, Knopf.

Becker, H. S. (1945) 'Interpretive sociology and constructive typology', in G. Gurvitch and W. E. Moore, eds, *Twentieth Century Sociology*, New York Philosophical Library.

Becker, H. S. (1951) 'The professional dance musician and his audience', *American Journal of Sociology*, vol. 57.

Becker, H. S. (1952) 'The career of the Chicago public school-teacher', *American Journal of Sociology*, vol. 57.

Becker, H. S. (1953) 'Becoming a marihuana user', *American Journal of Sociology*, vol. 59.

Becker, H. S. (1957) 'Participant observation and interviewing', *Human Organization*, Vol. 16.

Becker H. S. (1958) 'Problems of inference and proof in participant observation', *American Sociological Review*, vol. 23.

Becker, H. S. and Geer, B. (1960) 'Participant observation: the analysis of qualitative data', in R. N. Adams and J. J. Preiss, eds, *Human Organization Research*, Illinois, Dorsey Press.

Becker, H. S. and Strauss, A. L. (1956) 'Careers, personality and adult socialization', *American Journal of Sociology*, vol. 62.

Becker, H. S. *et al.* (1961) *Boys in White*, Chicago University Press.

Bendix, R. (1961) 'The image of man in the social sciences', in S. M. Lipset and N. Smelser, eds, *Sociology: the progress of a decade*, Prentice-Hall.

Berger, P. (1963) *Invitation to Sociology*, Doubleday-Anchor.

Bernal, J. D. (1969) *Science in History*, Penguin Books.

Bernard, L. L. (1945) 'The teaching of sociology in the United States in the last fifty years', *American Journal of Sociology*, vol. 50.

Blau, P. (1964) *Exchange and Power in Social Life*, Wiley.

Blumer, H. (1939) *Critiques of Research in the Social Sciences, I*, New York, S.S.R.C.

Bogardus, E. S. (1938) 'Social distance and its practical limitations', *Sociology and Social Research*, vol. 22.

Bogardus, E. S. (1963) 'Some pioneer American sociologists', *Sociology and Social Research*, vol. 47.

Booth, C. (1887) 'The inhabitants of the Tower Hamlets (School Board Division), their condition and occupations', *Journal of the Royal Statistical Society*, vol. 50.

Booth, C. (1902–3) Poverty Series.

Booth, C. (1902–3) Industry Series.

Booth, C. (1902–3) Religious Influences.

Booth, C., ed. (1892–97) *Life and Labour of the People of London*, 9 volumes, Macmillan.

Bottomore, T. B. and Rubel, M. (1963) *Karl Marx: Selected Writings*, Penguin Book, (Pelican).

Bowers R. V. (1958) 'Occupational roles of sociologists', *American Sociological Review*, vol. 23.

Bowley, A. L. and Bennet-Hurst, A. (1915a) *Livelihood and Poverty*, Bell.

Bowley, A. L. (1915b) *The Measurement of Social Phenomena*, P. S. King.

Bramson, L. (1961) *The Political Context of Sociology*, Princeton University Press.

Burgess, E. W. and Bogue, D., eds. (1964) *Contributions to Urban Sociology*, University of Chicago Press.

Burgess E. W., Bruce A. W. and Harno A. J., *The workings of the Indeterminate Sentence Law and the Parole System in Illinois: A Report to Honourable H. G. Clabaugh, Chairman of Board of Parole*, Chicago: Association for Criminal Justice, 1928.

Cavan, R. (1928) *Suicide*, University of Chicago Press.

Chadwick, E. (1842) *The Sanitary Condition of the Labouring Population of Great Britain*, ed. M. W. Flinn (1965), Edinburgh University Press; also see *New Society* series 'The origins of the social services' (1965).

Chapin, F. S. (1928) 'A quantitative scale for rating of the home and social environment of middle-class families in an urban environment', *Journal of Educational Psychology*, vol. 19.

Chapin, F. S. (1933) *The Measurement of Social Status*, Minneapolis.

Child, I. L. *et al.* (1946) 'Children's textbooks and personality development: an exploration in the social psychology of education', *Psychological Monographs*, vol. 60.

Colcord, J. C. (1939) *Your Community*, Russell Sage Foundation.

Commons, J. R. (1908) 'Standardization of housing investigations', *Journal of the American Statistical Association*, vol. 2.

Cotgrove, S. S. (1967) *Science of Society*, Allen & Unwin.

Cressey, P. G. (1932) *The Taxi Dance Hall*, University of Chicago Press.

Dalton, M. (1950) 'Conflict between staff and line managerial officers', *American Sociological Review*, vol. 15.

Dawe A. (1971) 'The two sociologies', in K. Thompson and J. Tunstall, eds, *Sociological Perspectives*, Penguin Books.

Duncan, H. G. and Duncan, W. L. (1933) 'Shifts in interests of American sociologists', *Social Forces*, vol. 12.

Durkheim, E. (1897) *Suicide*, repr. Routledge, 1952.

Durkheim, E. (1895) *The Rules of Sociological Method*, repr. New York, Free Press (1968).

Durkheim, E. (1912) *The Elementary Forms of the Religious Life*, trans. J. W. Swain, Allen & Unwin, 1915.

Engels, F. (1845) *The Conditions of the Working Class in England in 1844*, published in England in 1885.

Faris, R. E. L. (1967) *Chicago Sociology 1920–1932*, University of Chicago Press.

Firth, R. (1939) 'An anthropologist's view of mass observation', *Sociological Review*, vol. 31.

Frankenberg, R. (1966) *Communities in Britain*, Penguin Books.

Franz, J. G. (1939) 'Survey of sociometric techniques, with an annotated bibliography', *Sociometry*, vol. 2.

Fried, A. and Elman, R. M., eds (1969) *Charles Booth's London*, Hutchinson.

Friedrichs, R. W. (1970) *A Sociology of Sociology*, New York, Free Press.

Friedrichs, R. W. (1972) 'Dialectical sociology: an exemplar for the 1970s', *Social Forces*, vol. 50.

Friedrichs, R. W. (1972) 'Dialectical sociology: towards a resolution of the current "crisis" in Western sociology', *British Journal of Sociology*, vol. 13.

Fromm, E. (1942) *The Fear of Freedom*, Kegan Paul.

Garfinkel, H. (1967) *Studies in Ethnomethodology*, Prentice-Hall.

Geer B. (1964) 'First days in the field', in P. Hammond, ed. *Sociologists at Work*, Basic Books.

Giddings, F. H. (1910) 'Social marking system', *American Journal of Sociology*, vol. 15.

Glazer, N. (1959) 'The rise of social research in Europe', in D. Lerner, ed., *The Human Meaning of the Social Sciences*, New York, Meridian.

Glock, C. Y. (1967) *Survey Research in the Social Sciences*, New York, Russell Sage Foundations.

Glueck, E. and Glueck, S. (1950) *Unraveling Juvenile Delinquency*, New York, Commonwealth Fund.

Glueck, E. and Glueck, S. (1967) *Predicting Delinquency and Crime*, Harvard University Press.

Gottschalk, L., Kluckohn, C. and Angell, R. C. (1945) *The Use of Personal Documents in History, Anthropology and Sociology*, New York, S.S.R.C.

Gouldner, A. W. (1954) *Patterns of Industrial Bureaucracy*, New York, Free Press.

Gurvitch, G. and Moore, W. E. (1945) *Twentieth Century Sociology*, New York, Philosophical Library.

Hart, H. (1923) 'Predicting parole success', *Journal of Criminal Law and Criminology*, Vol. 14.

Hart, H. (1949) 'The pre-war upsurge in social science', *American Sociological Review*, vol. 14.

Hatt, P. K. (1950) 'Occupation and social stratification', *American Journal of Sociology*, vol. 55.

Herbertson, D. (1946) *The Life of Frederic Le Play*, ed. V. Brandford and A. Farquharson, Le Play House Press; reprinted as section 2 of vol. 38, *The Sociological Review*.

Hield, W. (1954) 'The study of change in social science', *British Journal of Sociology*, vol. 5.

Hinkle, R. C. and Hinkle, G. J. (1968) *The Development of Modern Sociology*, Random House.

Hobbs, A. H. (1951) *The Claims of Sociology: a critique of text-books*, Stockpole, Harrisburg, Telegraph Press.

Homans, G. C. (1951) *The Human Group*, Routledge & Kegan Paul.

Horowitz, I. L. (1965) 'The life and death of Project Camelot', *Trans-Action*.

Horowitz, I. L. (1968) *Professing Sociology*, Chicago, Aldine.

Hoselitz, B. F. (1959) 'The social sciences in the last two hundred years', in B. F. Hoselitz, ed. *A Reader's Guide to the Social Sciences*, New York, Free Press.

House, F. N. (1936) *The Development of Sociology*, McGraw-Hill.

Howerth, I. W. (1894) 'Present condition of sociology in the United States', *Annals of the American Academy of Political and Social Sciences*, vol. 5.

Hughes, E. C. (1964) 'Robert Park', *New Society*.

Jones, C. D. (1941) 'Evolution of the social survey in England since Booth', *American Journal of Sociology*, vol. 46.

Kahn, H. and Wiener, J. (1967) *The Year 2000*, Macmillan.

Katz, E. and Lazarsfeld, P. F. (1955) *Personal Influence*, New York, Free Press.

Kuhn, T. S. (1962) *The Structure of Scientific Revolutions*, University of Chicago Press.

Landsberger, H. A. (1958) *Hawthorne Revisited*, Cornell University Press.

Laswell, H. D. (1942) *Analysing the Contents of Mass Communication*, Document no. 11, Experimental Division for the Study of War Time Communications, Library of Congress, Washington, D.C.

Lazarsfeld, P. F. and Fiske, M. (1938) 'The Panel as a new tool for measuring opinion', *Public Opinion Quarterly*, Vol. 2.

Lazarsfeld, P. F., Berelson, B. and Gaudet H. (1948) *The People's Choice*, Columbia University Press.

Lazarsfeld, P. F. (1948) 'The use of panels in social research', *Proceedings of the American Philosophical Society*, vol. 42.

Lazarsfeld, P. F. (1962) 'The sociology of empirical social research', *American Sociological Review*, vol. 27.

Lenski, G. (1954) 'Status crystallization: a non-vertical dimension of social status', *American Sociological Review*, vol. 19.

Le Play, P. G. F. (1866) *La Reforme Sociale en France*, 2 vols, Paris, E. Dentu.

Lerner, D., ed. (1959) *The Human Meaning of the Social Sciences*, New York, Meridian.

Lewin, K. (1939) 'Experiments in social space', *Harvard Educational Review*, vol. 9.

Lewin K. (1947) 'Frontiers in group dynamics', *Human Relations*, vol. 1.

Lewin, K., Lippitt, R. and Escalona, S. K. (1940) 'An experimental study of the effect of democratic and authoritarian group atmospheres', in G. D. Stoddard, ed., *Studies in Topological and Vector Psychology*, no. 1, University of Iowa Press; also in *Studies in Child Welfare*, vol. 16.

Lewin, K., Lippitt, R. and White, R. K. (1939) 'Patterns of aggressive behaviour in experimentally created "social climates" ', *Journal of Social Psychology*, vol. 10; reprinted in D. S. Pugh, ed., *Organization Theory*, Penguin Books, 1971.

Lindeman, E. C. (1924) *Social Discovery*, New York, Republic.

Lippman, W. (1922) *Public Opinion*, Harcourt Brace.

Lipset, S. and Smelser, N. (1961) 'The setting of sociology in the 1950s', in Lipset and Smelser, eds., *Sociology: The Progress of a Decade*, Prentice-Hall.

Lundberg, G. A. (1929) *Social Research*, New York, Longmans.

Lundberg, G. A. (1930) 'The interests of members of the American Sociological Society, 1930', *American Journal of Sociology*, vol. 37.

Lundberg, G. A. (1945) 'The proximate future of American sociology: the growth of scientific method', *American Journal of Sociology*, vol. 50.

Lynd, R. S. and Lynd, H. M. (1929) *Middletown: a study in contemporary American culture*, Harcourt Brace.

McNemar, Q. (1946) 'Opinion attitude methodology', *Psychological Bulletin*, vol. 43.

Madge, J. (1963) *The Origins of Scientific Sociology*, Tavistock.

Malinowski, B. (1922) *Argonauts of the Western Pacific*, Routledge & Kegan Paul.

Manuel, F. E. (1965) *The Prophets of Paris*, Harper Torchbooks.

Marsak, L. M., ed. (1964) *The Rise of Science in Relation to Society*, Macmillan.

Martindale, D. (1964) 'The roles of humanism and scientism in the evolution of sociology', in G. K. Zollschan and W. Hirsch, eds, *Explorations in Social Change*, Houghton Mifflin.

Mass Observation (1937) *May 12th*, Faber.

Mass Observation (1938) *First Year's Work*, Lindsay Drummond.

Mass Observation (1938) *Britain*, Penguin Books.

Mass Observation (1940) *War Begins at Home*, Faber.

Mauss, H. (1962) *A Short History of Sociology*, Routledge & Kegan Paul.

Mayhew, H. (1851) *London Labour and the London Poor*, Griffin.

Meadows, D. H. *et al.* (1972) *The Limits to Growth*, Angus & Robertson.

Merton, R. K. and Lazarsfeld, P. F. (1951) *Continuities in Social Research*, New York, Free Press.

Mitchell G. D. (1968) *A Hundred Years of Sociology*, Duckworth.

Mitchell G. D. (1970) 'Sociology—an historical phenomenon', in P. Holmes, ed. *The Sociology of Sociology*, Sociological Review Monograph 16.

Moreno, J. L. (1934) *Who Shall Survive?*, Washington, D. C., Nervous and Mental Disease Publishing Co.

Mowrer, E. R. (1927) *Family Disorganisation*, University of Chicago Press.

Murphy, G., Murphy, L. B. and Newcomb, T. M. (1937) *Experimental Social Psychology*, Harper.

Myrdal, G. (1955) *The American Dilemma*, Harper.

Nettler, G. (1947) 'Toward a definition of the sociologist', *American Sociological Review*, vol. 12.

Newcomb, T. H. (1943) *Personality and Social Change*, New York, Dryden Press.

Newman, Sir George (1939) *The Building of a Nation's Health*, Macmillan.

Nisbet, R. (1966) *The Sociological Tradition*, Basic Books.

Norman, F. (1969) *Banana Boy*, Secker & Warburg; Corgi, 1970.

Odum, H. W. (1951) *American Sociology*, Longmans.

Ogburn, W. F. (1912) *Progress and Uniformity in Child Labor Legislation*, New York.

Ogburn, W. F. and Talbot, N. (1929) 'A measurement of the factors in the Presidential Election of 1928', *Social Forces*, vol. 18.

Ogburn, W. F. (1951) in Odum (1951) above.

Ogburn, W. F. and Odum H. W. (1934) *Recent Social Trends*, McGraw-Hill.

O'Neill, W. (1966) 'Divorce and the Professionalization of the Social Scientist', *Journal of the History of the Behavioral Sciences*, Vol. 2.

Oppenheimer, R. (1958) 'The growth of science and the structure of culture', *Daedalus*.

Ortega y Gassett, J. (1930) *Revolt of the Masses*, English edition, Allen & Unwin, 1932.

Park, R. E. (1915) 'The City: suggestions for the investigation of human behavior in an urban environment', *American Journal of Sociology*, vol. 20.

Park, R. E. (1924) 'A race relations survey', *Journal of Applied Sociology*.

Park, R. E. (1926) 'Methods of a race survey', *Journal of Applied Sociology*.

Park, R. E. (1929) 'The city as a social laboratory', in T. V. Smith and L. D. White, eds, *Chicago : an experiment in social science research*, University of Chicago Press.

Park, R. E. and Mears, E. G. (1925) 'Tentative findings of the Survey of Race Relations', from the unpublished 'Collected Papers of Robert Park', University of Chicago.

Parker, T. (1969) *The Twisting Lane*, Hutchinson.

Parker, T. (1970) *The Frying Pan : a prison and its prisoners*, Hutchinson.

Perry, C. A. (1913) 'A measure of the manner of living', *Quarterly Publication of American Statistical Association*, vol. 13.

Pfautz, H. W., ed. (1967) *Charles Booth on the City*, University of Chicago Press.

Pool, I. de Sola., ed. (1959) *Trends in Content Analysis*, University of Illinois Press.

Proshansky, H. and Seidenberg, B., eds, (1965) *Basic Studies in Social Psychology*, Holt, Rinehart & Winston.

Pugh, D. S. (1971) *Organization Theory*, Penguin Books.

Quetelet, J. A. L. (1846) *Sur la théorie de probabilité appliquée aux sciences morales et politiques*, Brussels, Hayez.

Raison, T., ed. (1969) *The Founding Fathers of Social Science*, Penguin Books.

Reckless, W. C. (1933) *Vice in Chicago*, University of Chicago Press.

Rex, J. A. (1970) 'The spread of the pathology of natural science to the social sciences', in P. Holmes, ed. *The Sociology of Sociology*, *Sociological Review* Monograph no. 16.

Riesman, D. *et al.* (1950) *The Lonely Crowd*, Yale University Press.

Rice, S. A. (1924) *Farmers and Workers in American Politics*, New York.

Rice, S. A. (1928) *Quantitative Methods in Politics*, Knopf.

Rice, S. A. (1931) *Methods in Social Science*, University of Chicago Press.

Rice, S. A. (1940) *Eleven Twenty-Six: A Decade of Social Science Research*, ed. Louis Wirth, Chicago University Press.

Riley, M. W. (1960) 'Membership of the American Sociological Association 1950–1959', *American Sociological Review*, vol. 25.

Roethlisberger, F. J. and Dickson W. J. (1939) *Management and the Worker*, Harvard University Press.

Rowntree, B. S. (1901) *Poverty: a study of town life*, Macmillan.

Roy, D. (1952) 'Quota restriction and goldbricking in a machine shop', *American Journal of Sociology*, vol. 57.

Seeley, J. R. (1963) 'Social science; some probative problems', in M. Stein and A. Vidich, eds, *Sociology on Trial*, Prentice-Hall.

Selvin, H. C. (1958) 'Durkheim's *Suicide* and the problems of empirical research', *American Journal of Sociology*, vol. 63.

Sewell, W. H. (1940) 'The construction and standardization of a scale for the measurement of the socio-economic status of Oklahoma farm families', *Technical Bulletin 9*, Oklahoma Agricultural and Mechanical College, Agricultural Experiment Station, Stillwater.

Shaw, C. R. (1930) *The Jack Roller*, University of Chicago Press; repr. Phoenix Books, 1967.

Shaw, C. R. (1931) *The Natural History of a Delinquent Career*, University of Chicago Press.

Shaw, C. R. (1938) *Brothers in Crime*, University of Chicago Press.

Shaw, C. R. and McKay, H. D. (1929) *Delinquency Areas*, University of Chicago Press.

Sherif, M. (1936a) *The Psychology of Social Norms*, Harper & Row.

Sherif, M. (1936b) 'Formation of social norms: the experimental paradigm', in H. Proshansky and B. Seidenberg, eds, *Basic Studies in Social Psychology*, Holt, Rinehart & Winston.

Shils, E. A. (1948) *The Present State of American Sociology*, New York, Free Press.

Simey, T. S. and Simey, M. B. (1960) *Charles Booth, Social Scientist*, Oxford University Press.

Simmel, G. (1902) 'The number of members as determining the sociological form of the group', *American Journal of Sociology*, vol. 8.

Sklair, L. (1970) *The Sociology of Progress*, Routledge.

Small, A. W. (1916) 'Fifty Years of sociology in the United States (1865–1915)', *American Journal of Sociology*, vol. 21.

Smith, T. V. and White, L. D., eds, (1929) *Chicago : an experiment in social science research*, University of Chicago Press.

Sorokin, P. A. (1937–41) *Social and Cultural Dynamics*, P. Owen.

Sorokin, P. A. (1965) 'Sociology of yesterday, today and tomorrow', *American Sociological Review*, vol. 30.

Sprott, W. J. H. (1952) *Social Psychology*, Methuen.

Stouffer, S. A. *et al.* (1950) *Measurement and Prediction*, Princeton University Press.

Thomas, W. I. and Znaniecki, F. (1927) *The Polish Peasant in Europe and America*, Knopf.

Thompson, K. (1972) 'The emergence of sociology', Unit 2 of The Open University Second Level Course, *The Sociological Perspective D283*.

Thrasher, F. M. (1927) *The Gang*, University of Chicago Press abridged edn with introduction by J. F. Short, Chicago, Phoenix Edition, 1963.

Thrasher, F. M. (1928) 'How to study the boys' gang in the open', *Journal of Educational Sociology*, vol. 1.

Tibbitts, H. G. (1962) 'Research in the development of sociology: a pilot study in methodology', *American Sociological Review*, Vol. 27.

de Tocqueville, A. (1835; 1945) ed. H. S. Commager, *Democracy in America*.

Townsend, P. (1957) *The Family Life of Old People*, Routledge.

Townsend, P. and Abel-Smith, B. (1965) *The Poor and the Poorest*, Bell.

Warner S. B. (1923) 'Factors determining parole from the Massachusetts Reformatory', *Journal of Criminal Law and Criminology*, vol. 14.

Warner, W. L. and Lunt, P. S. (1941) *The Social Life of a Modern Community*, Yale University Press.

Watson, J. D. (1968) *The Double Helix*, Weidenfeld & Nicolson.

Webb, S. and Webb, B. (1932) *Methods of Social Study*, repr. New York, Kelley, 1968.

Weber, M. (1949) *Methodology of the Social Sciences*, trans. E. Shils and H. Finch, New York, Free Press; a series of essays written between 1903 and 1917.

West, M. (1968) *The Tower of Babel*, Heinemann.

Whyte, W. F. (1943) *Street Corner Society*, University of Chicago Press.

Willcock, H. D. (1943) 'Mass observation', *American Journal of Sociology*, vol. 48.

Willey, M. M. (1926) *The Country Newspaper*, University of North Carolina Press/Oxford University Press.

Wirth, L. (1928) *The Ghetto*, University of Chicago Press.

Wirth, L., ed. (1940) *Eleven Twenty-Six*, University of Chicago Press.

Woofter, T. J. (1920) *Negro Migration: Changes in Rural Organization and Population of the Cotton Belt*, New York.

Young, D. R. (1927) 'Some effects of a course in American race problems on the race prejudices of 450 undergraduates at the University of Pennsylvania', *Journal of Abnormal Social Psychology*, vol. 22.

Young, K. (1931) 'Frederic M. Thrasher's study of gangs', in S. A. Rice, ed., *Methods in Social Science*, University of Chicago Press.

Young, K. (1962) 'The contribution of W. I. Thomas to sociology', *Sociology and Social Research*, vol. 47.

Young, P. (1939) *Scientific Social Surveys and Research*, Prentice-Hall.

Zetterberg, H. L., ed. (1956) *Sociology in the U.S.A.*, UNESCO.

Zilsel, E. (1964) 'The sociological roots of science', in H. Kearney, ed., *Origins of the Scientific Revolution*, Longmans.

Zimmerman, C. C. (1932) 'Ernst Engel's Law of Expenditure for Food', *Quarterly Journal of Economics*.

Zorbaugh, H. W. (1929) *The Gold Coast and the Slum*, University of Chicago Press.

Index

Sept. 1981